This book began as a simple wish to bring a taste of home to those of us who've wandered far from it, but it grew into something far richer thanks to the people around me.

To my family, for their endless patience and love while I filled the house with the smell of pickles, pastry, and photo props.

To Carl, for every lifted jar, late-night taste test (often of food he's not supposed to eat), and steady hand when mine was shaking. And to my children, who have been both my reason and my reminder that love takes many shapes.

To Janine, my marketing guru and voice of clarity when my own wavered, thank you for helping me see the bigger picture and believe this little dream could reach far beyond my kitchen table.

To the local growers and makers who share their produce and stories so generously, and to the expats who've shared their own memories with me along the way, you're all part of this feast.

And lastly, to Mum and Dad. Everything I cook, write, and create begins and ends with you.

Contents

Introduction
Don't Rush It. All Good Things Come to Those 4
Who Wait 6
Kitchen Tips for Easier Baking 7
A Little Laugh From My Oven To Yours 9
Making Time For Baking 10
Conversion Charts 11

Sauces & Pickles 12

Bourbon BBQ Sauce 15
Cranberry, Port & Orange Sauce 17
Classic Piccalilli 19
Farmhouse Pickle 22
Gravy 23
Homemade Tomato Sauce 24
Mint Sauce 26
Merry Figgin' Christmas Jam 27
Nan's Pickled Onions 29
Pickled Red Cabbage 30
Special Burger Sauces 31

More Than Just Veg 34

Easy Ways to Take Humble Veg 37
from Sidekick - to Showstopper
Brussels Sprouts With Walnut & Blue Cheese 38
Mashed Brussels Sprouts with Garlic & Parmesan 39
Cauliflower Cheese 41
Roasted Butternut Squash & Cumin Soup 43
The Perfect Roasties 44
Roasted Cauliflower with Lemon, Cumin & Coriander 47
Sautéed Cabbage with Bacon 49

The Butcher, The Baker & The Breakfast Maker 50

Bacon & Egg Sandwich 53
Breakfast Pies 55
Bubble & Squeak 57
Homemade British Back Bacon 59
Irish Potato Farls 61
Kedgeree 63
Our Bakery-Style Cheese & Bacon Wrap 65
Savoury Pancake Stack 67
Sausage, Bean & Cheese Melt 69
Brekky Burritos 70

Pies & Pastries 71

Cheese & Onion Pasty 75
Chicken Slice 76
The Great British Steak Slice 77
Our Bakery Pork Sausage Roll 79
Our Bakery Pork Pie 81
Pork & Egg Pie (Stand Pie) 83
Pie, Mash & Liquor 84
Cornish Pasty 87
Football, Pies & Expat Life **88**
Traditional Scotch Pies 91
Killie Pie 92
Chicken Balti Pie 93
Peppery Minced Beef Pie 94

Picnics & Sandwiches 95

Croque Monsieur 98
Reuben Toastie 99
Tandoori Chicken Sandwich 101
How to Build a Salad 102
Quick & Easy Homemade Salad 103
Cheese & Onion Quiche **105**
Our Bakery Scotch Eggs 107
Classic Chicken Shawarma 108
Sandwich Fillers **109**
Cheese & Onion Sandwich Filler 111
Chicken, Mayo & Sweetcorn 112
Sandwich Filler Coronation 113
Chicken Tikka Sandwich Filler 115
Prawn Cocktail Sandwich Filler 116
Tuna Crunch Sandwich Filler 117

Cakes & Baking 118

Cherry Bakewell Muffins 121
Belgian Buns 122
Battenberg Cake 124
Chelsea Buns 127
Millionaire's Shortbread 129
Eccles Cakes 131
Jamaican Ginger Cake 133
Melton Hunt Cake 135
Our Bakery Scones 137
Traditional Almond Slice 139
Victoria Sponge 141
Yorkshire Tea Loaf 143
Yum Yums 145

Puddings & Desserts — 146

- Clotted Cream or Not Clotted Cream? — 149
- Blackberry & Apple Cobbler — 151
- Bread & Butter Pudding — 153
- Classic British Trifle — 155
- Chocolate Crunch — 157
- Mum's Treacle Tart — 159
- Queen of Puddings — 160
- Raspberry Fool with Mascarpone — 163
- Traditional Custard Tarts — 165
- A Viennetta Style Dessert — 166

Christmas & Entertaining — 167

Party Food & Tipples — 169
- Brie en Croute — 171
- Festive Slice — 173
- Goat's Cheese Log — 175
- Homemade Herbed Cheese Bites — 177
- Mini Yorkies with rare roast beef & horseradish — 179
- Vol-au-Vents — 181
- Gingerbread — 183
- Homemade Sweet Mincemeat — 185
- Mulled Wine or Cider — 187
- Homemade Irish Cream — 189

Grazing Boards Party Food Prep Guide — 190
- Party Food Prep Guide — 191
- Grazing Boards — 192
- Mini Grazing Cups — 194
- Easy & Impressive Party Food Ideas — 195

The Main Event — 196
- Christmas Prawn Cocktail — 199
- Braised Red Cabbage with Apple — 200
- Honey Roasted Parsnips — 201
- Brussels Sprouts with Pancetta & Almonds — 203
- Chicken, Bacon & Stuffing Hot Water Crust Pie — 204
- Pigs in Blankets — 207
- Roast Turkey, British Butcher Style — 208
- Sage & Onion Stuffing — 210
- Traditional Christmas Pudding — 211
- Yule Log — 213

Eating In Like You're Eating Out — 215

Pub Classics — 217
- Proper Fish & Chips — 218
- Steak & Kidney Pudding — 221
- Stuffed Roast Pork Loin — 223
- Giant Yorkshire Pudding — 225
- Yorkshire Pudding Wrap — 226

Curry Night In — 227
- Chicken Tikka Masala — 228
- Lamb Rogan Josh — 231
- Homemade Naan — 233
- Onion Bhajis — 234

Bistro & Grill Favourites — 235
- Bistecca Al Pomodoro — 236
- Flame-Grilled Burger — 237
- Chicken Cordon Bleu — 239
- Sticky Bourbon BBQ Ribs — 241
- Lamb Chops with Garlic & Herbs — 242

Little Chefs' Big Flavours — 243

- Easy Peasy Flapjacks — 245
- Cheesy Meatballs — 247
- That's a Wrap (Yo Chicken Style) — 249
- Crispy Southern Fried Chicken — 251
- Fakeaway Flame-Grilled Patties — 252
- Let's Make Pizza — 255
- Mac & Cheese — 257
- Sausage & Egg Brekky Muffin — 259

Introduction

Cookbooks line my kitchen shelf, though most rarely see daylight. A few gather dust, waiting, while others are bound for the Salvos. On baking days, three or four leap into action, propped between mixing bowls and cooling racks on my ever-cluttered worktop.

I was born in Bristol, in the southwest of England, but it was love that took me north and into a new world of flavour. After meeting Carl, a proud Yorkshireman, I discovered hearty comfort dishes,
rich gravies, cosy puddings and proper pies that became staples in my kitchen. Now we live in Perth Australia with our children and our four-legged sous chef, Lilo.

Like many expats, we have spent years chasing the flavours of home, hunting for ingredients, tweaking recipes and recreating the tastes that tie us to our roots. Biting into a flaky pastry or spooning up a proper roast is not just about food; it's about belonging.

My cooking journey in Perth began after my breast cancer diagnosis in 2020. I was running a small dressmaking business, creating by hand and always chasing perfection, until the diagnosis forced me to slow down. What felt like an ending soon became a beginning. Encouraged by Carl to find something gentler, I turned to baking. It started as therapy, then joy, and before long, I was sending platters of sweets and savouries to his colleagues, perfecting pork pies and falling in love with the process. What began as a kitchen hobby grew into The Yorkshireman's Pie, our little British bakery that was here in Perth, and from there, this book.

Food has always been my way of connecting with people, places, and memories. I can still see myself perched on the step of Dad's fruit and veg lorry, sneaking sweet peas as Mum prepared Sunday roasts that smelled like home. Every recipe in this book carries a piece of that story, a taste of family, comfort, and tradition shared.

This book is for anyone who loves simple, honest cooking, the kind that fills your home with warmth and brings people together. You do not have to be an expat to understand that pull toward familiar flavours. From Australia to Canada, Ireland to South Africa, we all share a taste for comfort — golden pies, rich gravies, and roasts that evoke a sense of Sunday. No matter where you live, those recipes carry a little piece of home.

Even if pork pies or pickled onions were never part of your childhood, something here will feel familiar. Maybe it's a flavour, a memory, or simply the joy of making food from scratch. Because food should be more than just fuel, it should remind us who we are and where we have come from.
So tie on your apron, call over the dog, and gather those you love. Let's make something extraordinary, one recipe at a time.

Linda x

Don't Rush It. All Good Things Come To Those Who Wait.

"It's tempting to rush when you're eager to eat. But the magic lives in those extra steps:

Letting the dough rest, watching it rise, creaming butter and sugar just so. They're not filler; they're what gives your baking flavour, texture, and character.

Rest the Pastry

Chilling relaxes the gluten in the flour and firms the fat, giving flaky, tender results. Skip it, and you get tough pastry.

Let the Dough Rise

Yeast needs time to work, creating bread that's light, airy and full of flavour. Rush it, and the final product will be dense (a bit like a house brick).

Rest the Yorkshire Pudding Batter

Resting gives the flour time to hydrate. A rest gives the starch time to swell making the batter smoother and more even.

Cream Butter and Sugar

Creaming traps air, giving a fine crumb and even sweetness. Mix until pale and fluffy.

Choose Butter

Butter's higher fat content provides richer flavour and more consistent results. Margarine or other spreads can't match it.

Trust the Process

Take your time and let the steps, resting, rising, and creaming, do their work. Patience always rewards you with better baking

Kitchen Tips for Easier Baking

Salt in the Egg Wash

Add a tiny pinch of salt to your egg wash to break down egg proteins, making it easier to brush on, giving pastry an even, golden finish

Easier Egg Peeling

Tap the wide end of a boiled egg (where the air pocket is) and peel under running water.

Keep Herbs Fresh for Longer

Stand parsley or coriander (cilantro) in a glass of water (like a bouquet), cover loosely with a plastic bag, and store in the fridge.

Peel Garlic Easily

Smash a garlic clove with the flat side of a knife, and the skin will slip right off.

Fluffier Scrambled Eggs

For soft, fluffy scrambled eggs, add a splash of cold water to create steam as they cook.

Test Your Baking Powder

Stir a teaspoon of baking powder into hot water. If it fizzes, it's still fresh. If not, use a new tin.

Prevent Boil-Overs

Lay a wooden spoon across the top of your pot while boiling pasta to break bubbles and prevent overflow.

Stop Your Chopping Board from Slipping

Tuck a damp tea towel or paper towel underneath your chopping board to hold it steady while you chop.

No Buttermilk, No Problem

Mix 240ml milk with 15ml (1 tablespoon) lemon juice or vinegar. Let it sit for 5 minutes for instant buttermilk.

And Finally ...

Proving dough? Use a shower cap. A cheap shower cap is perfect for covering your proving bowls.
As Del Boy Trotter would put it in Only Fools and Horses:

"Bonnet de douche, Rodney, bonnet de douche!"

— French for shower cap, and perfectly practical in the kitchen too.

A Little Laugh From My Oven To Yours

Cooking should feel like an adventure, not a test. Whether you're an experienced home cook or just finding your
way around the kitchen, don't stress about perfect techniques or fancy ingredients.
This book is all about bringing joy back to the cooking experience. I want you to create food that feels good, tastes great, and brings people together.
Each recipe is simple, satisfying, and designed for proper kitchens. I use ingredients you can find in your pantry or at a local shop, with a few tips to make everyday dishes even better. You don't need a Michelin star, just curiosity and a clean apron.
Of course, not every kitchen adventure runs perfectly. No cook, however experienced, avoids the odd mishap.
If things go wrong, you're in very good company.
Here are a few of my favourites (yes, most are mine) to lighten the mood when recipes don't turn out
as planned.

The Salt–Sugar Switcheroo

Measuring what you think is sugar, only to find out after serving that it was salt.

Plastic Meltdown

Microwaving leftovers with the lid still sealed, only to end up with a Salvador Dalí-inspired sculpture. Or roasting a spatula alongside the roasties. Happens more than you'd think.

The Flour Cloud

I once started the mixer too soon and aged forty years in four seconds. A flour facial keeps you humble.

The Smoke Alarm Starter Pistol

At our house, dinner begins when the smoke alarm goes off. Keep a tea towel handy to flap or mop up.

Did I Add that Already?

You add bicarbonate; wonder if you've already done so, then add more. Now your cake erupts and tastes like soap

The Great Pasta Flood

Leave pasta alone for a minute, and the stove top becomes a foaming cauldron. The dog? Ecstatic.

Unintended Defrosting

You meant to turn on the oven. After 45 minutes, dinner sat in a cold box. Takeaway it is.

Making Time For Baking

Most People simply don't have the time to spend hours in the kitchen amid their busy lives. This book is here to tempt you to set aside a Saturday or Sunday for your own British Bake Off day, showing you how to make it feel both special and entirely doable.

Pick a Theme
Try Scone Saturday, Pudding Perfection, or Pies & Pastries. Choosing a theme for your baking day makes it feel special and gives you a fun focus for what to bake.

Keep it Simple
Not everything needs to be a showstopper. Scones, jam tarts, or a Victoria sponge are all quick and satisfying options.

Enjoy the Process
Put on your favourite playlist, pour a cuppa, and embrace the floury mess

Bake Once, Enjoy All Week
Think of it as meal-prepping for your sweet tooth.

Share the Joy!
If you are a bit of a photography tart like me, show off your creation on social media!

Try... #Britishbakesaturday or #Saturdaybakeclub #porkpiesandtheperfectpickle and #tasteofhome to find your people.
Because food's always better when shared.

Conversion Charts

Here's a handy conversion chart for common kitchen measurements in cups, grams, and ounces

Ingredients	1 Cup (US)	Grams	Ounces
Flour	1	120	4.2
Sugar	1	200	7
Butter	1	227	8
Milk/cream	1	240	8.5
Parmesan Cheese	1	90	3.2
Cheese grated	1	100	3.5
Rice (uncooked)	1	200	7
Oats (Rolled)	1	90	3.2
Water	1	240	8.5
Yoghurt	1	240	8.5
Nuts (chopped)	1	130	4.6
Cocoa Powder	1	85	3

Celsius (°C)	Fahrenheit (°F)	Gas Mark
110 °C	230 °F	1/4
120 °C	250 °F	1/2
150 °C	300 °F	2
160 °C	325 °F	3
170 °C	340 °F	4
180 °C	350 °F	4-5
190 °C	375 °F	5
200 °C	400 °F	6
220 °C	425 °F	7
230 °C	450 °F	8
240 °C	475 °F	9

General Conversions

1 cup = 240 millilitres (ml)
1 gram = 0.035 ounces (oz)
1 ounce = 28.35 grams (g)

Sauces & Pickles

> *"Just a dollop on t'side to go wi' me pork pie. My uncle Jack and I loved pork pies, with a bit of brown sauce on the side."*
>
> – Joanna Sisco

My mum was the kind of cook who could have six pans bubbling, meat resting, veg steaming, and still manage to get gravy on her back. No one knows how. She never even flinched. A domestic miracle, or a woman who never let a bit of splatter get in the way of feeding people properly.

In this chapter, I've gathered the sauces and pickles that bring a meal to life. They are the ones that run down Sunday plates, turn a simple Tuesday tea into something posh, or rescue dinners that didn't quite go as planned.

The battle over the 'correct' sauce is never-ending. Some swear by mint with lamb, while others insist that only red sauce belongs on a fry-up. In truth, the right sauce is the one that makes your plate sing. Sauces and pickles are the unsung heroes of the dinner table, elevating everything from a humble pork pie to a burger straight off the BBQ. They add depth, texture, and that extra kick that transforms a meal from "nice" to "bloody fantastic."

Sure, store-bought sauces are convenient, and I won't pretend I don't have a few guilty pleasures (HP, I'm looking at you). But nothing beats homemade, where you set the spice and sweetness, and best of all, there are no mystery ingredients: no preservatives, no numbers on a label, just honest flavours.

Living in Australia, we make the most of the outdoor lifestyle, which means our BBQ gets a fair amount of use. Burgers are a staple in our house, and I always have a big batch of homemade burger sauce ready to go. Why buy a tiny 250 g jar from the shop when you can whip up a vat of the good stuff at home?

So, whether you're a brown sauce devotee, a pickle connoisseur, or someone who loves a proper dollop of something tasty on the side, this chapter is for you. Get ready to dip, dunk, and drizzle your way through some of the best homemade sauces and pickles you'll ever taste.

Bourbon BBQ Sauce
Rich, smoky, and tangy, perfect brushed on ribs, grilled chicken, or stirred into mayo.

Cranberry, Port & Orange Sauce
A glossy, ruby sauce that brings Christmas to the table, just as good with turkey as with Brie in a crusty roll.

Classic Piccalilli
Tangy mustard, crunchy vegetables, a pinch of turmeric, the ultimate Ploughman's pickle.

Farmhouse Pickle
A homemade take on Branston. Chunky vegetables, sweet and tangy, a natural with cheese

Merry Figgin' Christmas Jam
Fresh figs from the garden, honey from the bees, sticky spiced and glorious with cheese

Gravy (or Pan Jus, If You're Wearing Pearls)
Proper roasting-pan gravy, no granules, just instinct, patience, and Sunday lunch memories.

Mint Sauce
Freshly picked from the garden, chopped and stirred with sugar and vinegar, just as Mum made it.

Nan's Pickled Onions
Sharp, spiced, and crisp, the smell of vinegar in Nan's kitchen, jars lined up for Christmas

Pickled Red Cabbage
Bright pink, bold, and bossy, the perfect bite with pork pie, ham, or cheddar

Special Burger Sauces
Two styles side by side. Flame-grilled depth or classics special sauce tang.

Homemade Tomato Sauce (Ketchup)
Better than shop-bought, full of spice and depth, whether sparingly dipped or lavishly drenched.

Bourbon BBQ Sauce

This sauce is rich and smoky, with just enough sweetness to balance its tang. It's a proper BBQ companion, bold without being over the top. Brush it over ribs, steak, or chicken, or stir a spoonful into mayo for a spirited sandwich spread. I also use this as the glaze in my Sticky Bourbon BBQ Ribs (see the chapter 'Eat In Like You're Eating Out' in this book), where it caramelises into a glossy, finger-licking finish.

Makes: Approx 500 ml
Cook Time: 20 min
Total Time: 25 min
Prep Time: 5 min

Ingredients

240g ketchup (Tomato Sauce recipe in this chapter)
120ml bourbon
60ml apple cider vinegar
45g brown sugar
2 tablespoons Worcestershire sauce
2 tablespoons Dijon mustard
1 tablespoon smoked paprika
1 tablespoon garlic powder
1 tablespoon onion powder
1 teaspoon ground black pepper
½ teaspoon cayenne pepper (optional, for heat)
½ teaspoon salt

Method

Place all ingredients in a medium saucepan over medium heat.
Stir until sugar dissolves.
Reduce heat and simmer 20-30 minutes, stirring occasionally, until thickened.
Taste and adjust salt, sugar, or cayenne as needed. For a thinner sauce, add a splash of water or vinegar. Cool slightly before serving with grilled meats, burgers, or vegetables.

Tips

For a deeper bourbon flavour, add a little extra
and reduce for a longer period

Storage & Reheating

Cool completely before storing. Keep in a sterilised jar or airtight container in the fridge for up to 2 weeks.

Reheating: Gently reheat in a small saucepan over low heat, stirring occasionally, until the sauce is warm.
If the sauce has thickened in the fridge, loosen with a splash of water, vinegar, or bourbon before serving.

Cranberry, Port & Orange Sauce

Cranberry, Port & Orange Sauce

The first time I tasted this cranberry sauce was just before Christmas, when my husband brought home a jar from the Chatsworth House farm shop in Derbyshire. Rich with port, bright with orange, and beautifully tart, it was a revelation, far superior to any cranberry sauce I'd had before. This version is my homage to that stately home treat. A glossy, ruby-red sauce, perfect for turkey on Christmas Day or tucked into a crusty roll with Brie the next day.

Makes: 1 jar (about 250 g)
Prep Time: 5 minutes
Cook Time: Approx 15 minutes
Total Time: 15–20 minutes

Ingredients

250g fresh or frozen cranberries
150g sugar
150ml ruby port
Juice and zest of 1 orange
½ teaspoon ground cinnamon
Pinch of salt

Method

1. Place cranberries, sugar, port, orange juice, zest, cinnamon, and salt in a medium saucepan.
2. Heat gently over medium heat, stirring until sugar dissolves and cranberries begin to burst (about 10–12 minutes).
3. Reduce heat and simmer for 3–5 minutes until the sauce thickens.
4. Remove from heat and allow to cool slightly; the sauce will thicken further as it cools. Serve warm or at room temperature with roasted meats

Tips

For a smoother sauce, pulse briefly in a blender once cooled.

Storage

Cool completely before storing. Keep in a sterilised jar in the fridge for up to 2 weeks.

Classic Piccalilli

Classic Piccalilli

English piccalilli reigns supreme among pickles. With its tangy mustard base and vibrant mix of cauliflower, gherkins, and onions, it delivers a bold, zesty flavour. The sharp mustard and turmeric cut through the richness, making it perfect with cold meats, cheeses, or a ploughman's lunch. It also shines as a sandwich spread or spooned over roasted vegetables for a lively twist.

Makes: 4–5 jars (250 g each) **Cook Time:** 1 hour **Total Time:** 1 hour 30 minutes (plus 24 hours resting)

Prep Time: 30 minutes

Ingredients

500g cauliflower florets
200g zucchini (courgette) or gherkins, diced
200g shallots or white onions, chopped
600ml malt vinegar
3 tablespoons English mustard powder
1 tablespoon coriander seeds
2 tablespoons mustard seeds
2 teaspoons cumin seeds
1 teaspoon ground turmeric
4 tablespoons plain flour
200g caster sugar
2 bay leaves
Salt, to taste

Method

Rest the Vegetables.
Combine cauliflower, zucchini, and onions in a large bowl. Sprinkle with salt, mix well, cover with a clean tea towel, and leave in a cool place for 24 hours. Rinse thoroughly with water and drain well.

Make the Spiced Vinegar
In a saucepan, combine vinegar, mustard powder, coriander seeds, mustard seeds, cumin seeds, turmeric, and bay leaves. Bring to the boil, then simmer for 5 minutes.
In a small bowl, mix flour with a little water to form a paste.
Stir the paste into the vinegar mixture, whisking constantly, until thickened. Add sugar and stir until dissolved.

Cook and Jar

Stir in the vegetables and cook for an additional 5 minutes.
Remove bay leaves and spoon into sterilised jars while warm.

Storage

Store in sterilised jars in a cool, dark place for at least 2 weeks before eating. Flavour improves if matured for longer (e.g., 1 month).
Will keep unopened for up to 1 year. Once opened, refrigerate and use within 6 weeks.

"Bring out the Branston!"

Remember that jingle? Few things feel more like home than this iconic British favourite. Branston Pickle has graced sandwiches, pies, and cheeseboards for decades.
Whether paired with a ploughman's lunch or tucked into a cheese sandwich, its sweet-and-spicy balance really shines.

Farmhouse Pickle

While you can still buy a jar from the supermarket, nothing beats making your own. This version captures that robust flavour, and you'll be ready to perk up anything that needs an extra kick.

Makes: 4 jars (250 g each)

Prep Time: 40 minutes (plus 1–2 hours optional resting)

Cook Time: 1 hour

Total Time: 1 hour 40 minutes (1–2 hours optional resting) 2 weeks to mature

Ingredients

300g carrots, peeled and finely diced
300g swede (rutabaga), peeled and finely diced
200g onion, finely chopped
150g cauliflower, cut into tiny florets
100g apple, peeled and diced
100g dates, finely chopped (or use raisins for a more old-fashioned feel)
1 clove garlic, crushed
1 tablespoon salt
1 tablespoon English mustard powder
1 teaspoon ground allspice
½ teaspoon ground cinnamon
¼ teaspoon ground cloves
350ml malt vinegar
200g soft brown sugar
1 tablespoon black treacle (optional, deepens flavour)
1 tablespoon cornflour for thickening

Method

Rest the Vegetables
Place all the chopped vegetables in a large bowl, sprinkle with salt, and toss well. Cover and leave to rest for 1–2 hours. Rinse thoroughly and drain well before using.

Make the Spiced Vinegar and Cook
In a heavy pan, combine the vinegar, sugar, garlic, spices treacle, and mustard powder. Bring to a gentle boil, then reduce the heat and simmer for 5 minutes.

Add the prepared vegetables along with the apple and dates. Simmer gently, uncovered, for 1–1 hour 30 minutes, until the vegetables are tender but not mushy and the liquid has reduced.

Thicken and finish.
Mix the cornflour with one tablespoon of cold water to form a paste. Stir into the pickle and cook for a few minutes more, until the mixture is glossy and rich.

Spoon the hot pickle into sterilised jars, seal, and leave to mature for at least 2 weeks. For the fullest flavour, give it a month before opening.

Storage

Pour while hot into sterilised jars. Seal and leave to mature for at least 2 weeks, ideally 1 month.
Will keep unopened in a cool, dark cupboard for up to 1 year. Once opened, refrigerate and use within 6 weeks.

Gravy

(or Pan-Jus if you're wearing pearls)

Gravy may seem a minor detail, but for many living away from home, it's special. It doesn't just tie the roast dinner together; it brings back memories of Sunday lunch, the scent of something simmering, vegetables bubbling, and Mum stirring the pans with purpose.
It's never been about instant granules. This is the genuine stuff: made in the roasting pan, thickened traditionally with vegetable water and meat juices. No teaspoons of powder, just instinct, patience, and stirring while half-watching Songs of Praise on the television on Sunday.

Makes: Approx 400 ml **Cook Time:** 10 minutes **Total Time:** 12 minutes
Prep Time: 2 minutes

Ingredients

2 tablespoons drippings from the roast (or oil/vegetarian fat)
2 tablespoons plain flour (or gluten-free flour blend/cornflour)
200ml vegetable water (from cooked vegetables) or vegetable stock
1-2 tablespoons gravy browning (liquid seasoning to darken gravy, optional)
Salt and freshly ground black pepper

Method

Melt drippings in a pan over medium heat. Stir in flour and cook for two minutes, stirring constantly.
Gradually pour in vegetable water or stock, whisking as you go. Bring to a gentle simmer.
Stir until gravy thickens and coats the back of a spoon. If too thick, add more liquid.
Add gravy browning for colour, if desired. Season with salt and pepper.
A splash of Worcestershire sauce also adds depth

Adaptations & Substitutions

Parisian Essence: (Australia & NZ): Caramel-coloured burnt sugar liquid; start with ½–1 teaspoon.
Worcestershire sauce: Adds depth and tang.
Kitchen Bouquet (USA): Close to UK browning.
Black treacle or molasses: ¼ teaspoon adds colour and sweetness, especially with lamb or beef.
Add gradually. Once the colour is in, you can't take it out!

Storage & Reheating

Cool completely, then transfer to an airtight container.
Refrigerate for up to 3 days or freeze for up to 3 months.
Reheating: Reheat gently, adding water or stock if too thick.

Homemade Tomato Sauce
(Ketchup)

Ketchup: the great divider. Some use it sparingly with a fry-up or chips. Others, like my son, believed every meal benefited from a drenching, even a Sunday roast. Homemade ketchup, however, surpasses any shop-bought version: full of love, spice, and depth of flavour.

Makes: Approx 300 ml

Prep Time: 5 minutes

Cook Time: 25–30 minutes

Total Time: 30–35 minutes

Ingredients

1 × 400g tin chopped tomatoes or passata
2 tablespoons tomato paste
1 small onion, finely chopped
2 tablespoons white vinegar
1 tablespoon brown sugar (adjust to taste)
1 tablespoon mustard powder
1 tablespoon ground ginger
½ teaspoon ground allspice
½ teaspoon paprika (smoked, if desired)
¼ teaspoon ground cinnamon
¼ teaspoon ground cloves
½ teaspoon salt (adjust to taste)
¼ teaspoon black pepper (optional, adjust to taste)
vegetable oil for frying

Method

Heat a splash of oil in a medium saucepan over medium heat.
Cook onion until soft and translucent, about 5 minutes.
Stir in chopped tomatoes, tomato paste, and vinegar. Bring to a gentle simmer.
Stir in sugar, mustard powder, ginger, allspice, paprika, cinnamon, cloves, salt, and black pepper. Simmer for 25– 30 minutes stirring occasionally, until thickened.
Allow to cool, then blend until smooth with a stick blender or food processor. For a rustic sauce, mash lightly or leave chunky.
Taste and balance with more sugar for sweetness or vinegar for tang.
Cool to room temperature before transferring to a jar or bottle.

Adaptations & Substitutions

Heat: Add cayenne or hot sauce for extra warmth.
Tang: Swap in apple cider vinegar for a fruity sharpness.
Smoke: Add roasted garlic or chipotle powder for a rich, smoky depth.

Storage

Keep in a sterilised jar or airtight container in the fridge for up to 2 weeks.

Mint Sauce

Mint sauce is more than just a tangy accompaniment to a roast. Mum used to head out to the garden, gather a bunch of fresh mint, and then set about chopping, stirring sugar into vinegar, and letting the whole kitchen fill with that bright, refreshing scent. It brought life to lamb, chicken, beef, or buttery new potatoes, and no shop-bought version has ever come close. Spearmint gives a gentle, sweet aroma, while peppermint adds a sharper kick.

Makes: 4-6 servings

Cook Time: 5 minutes

Total Time: 15 minutes

Prep Time: 10 minutes

Ingredients

A good handful of fresh mint leaves
1 tablespoon sugar
2 tablespoons boiling water
2-3 tablespoons malt vinegar

Method

Finely chop the mint leaves. Stir in sugar, then add boiling water. Mix until the sugar has dissolved. Pour in vinegar, adjusting to taste. Leave to cool for 1 hour at room temperature, or 30 minutes in the fridge, before serving. The flavour will deepen further if left overnight.

Adaptations & Substitutes

If fresh mint isn't available, use half the amount of dried mint, soaking it briefly in vinegar to rehydrate. Herb pastes are useful in a pinch.

Storage

Store in a clean, airtight container in the fridge for up to 2 weeks. If sauce thickens, loosen with a splash of hot water or extra vinegar before serving.

Merry Figgin' Christmas Jam

This isn't your everyday British jam. I have a fig tree in the garden here in Perth, and when the fruit is in season, it practically throws itself at me. We also keep a beehive, so I use honey from the bees, which gives the jam a rich, floral sweetness. With the figs and honey, this conserve is sticky, luscious, and lightly spiced. Perfect on toast, stirred into porridge, or served with cheese, it captures the essence of summer and cosy autumn afternoons.

Makes: 2-3 jars (250g) **Cook Time:** 40-50 minutes **Total Time:** 50-60 minutes

Prep Time: 10 minutes

Ingredients

500g fresh figs, trimmed and quartered
200g caster sugar
100g runny honey
(or maple syrup, or an extra 50g sugar if avoiding honey)
Juice of 1 lemon
1 teaspoon ground cinnamon
¼ teaspoon ground cloves
50ml water

Method

Combine figs, sugar, honey, lemon juice spices, and water in a large pan.

Stir gently over medium heat until the sugar dissolves, then bring to a gentle boil. Simmer uncovered for 40-50 minutes, stirring occasionally, until the figs have broken down and the jam has thickened to a spreadable consistency.

Test by placing a spoonful on a cold plate. If it sets when pressed, it's ready. If not, simmer longer or add a touch more lemon juice and continue cooking.

Remember, the jam will thicken slightly as it cools.

Pour into sterilised jars while warm, seal, and allow to cool.

Spread on warm toast or crumpets.

Spoon onto a cheese board—Brie and blue cheese pair beautifully.

Stir into Greek yoghurt or porridge.

Adaptations & Substitutes

If fresh figs aren't available, soak dried figs in water for a few hours before use.

Sterilising Jars: Boil jars in water for 10 minutes or place in a preheated oven at 150°C for 20minutes

Storage

Store unopened jars in a cool, dark place for up to 1 year. In humid climates, store jam in a cool, dark place and check for signs of mould or fermentation. A good seal is essential. Once opened, keep refrigerated and use within 1 month.

Nan's Pickled Onions

Homemade pickled onions are more than a condiment. They are a tradition, part of Christmas or pub lunches, not just a topping. Their crisp crunch, sharp tang, and warming spice make them irresistible, while the aroma of malt vinegar heating brings back memories of family gatherings filled with laughter. Nan prepared them early for Christmas, the jars maturing on the shelf and filling the house with the sharp scent of vinegar. By the time December rolled around, they were at their best, a nostalgic treat that still feels like home.

Makes: 4-5 medium jars

Prep Time: 30 minutes

Cook Time: 5 minutes

Total Time: 35 minutes (plus 2-6 weeks pickling)

Ingredients

1 kg small pickling onions or shallots

100g salt

1 litre malt vinegar (or spiced pickling vinegar)

2 tablespoons brown sugar

1 tablespoon pickling spice (or a mix of mustard seeds, peppercorns, coriander seeds, dried chilli, and bay leaf)

Prepare Onions

Peel onions (soaking briefly in hot water makes this easier). Place in a bowl (they should sit in a non-reactive bowl, such as glass, ceramic, or stainless steel). Sprinkle with salt, cover with a clean tea towel or cling wrap, and leave overnight. This draws out moisture and keeps them crunchy.

Rinse onions in cold water and pat dry.
In a saucepan, gently heat vinegar, brown sugar, and pickling spice. Do not boil. Warm just enough to dissolve sugar and blend flavours, then allow to cool.
Pack onions into sterilised jars. Completely cover the onions with cooled vinegar, then seal the jars

Tips

Use robust malt vinegar for a traditional flavour. Don't skip the salting step; it ensures crunch. Adjust spice mix to taste; a pinch of dried chilli adds warmth. Patience is key. The longer they mature, the richer the taste.

Adaptations & Substitutions

Lighter Flavour: Swap malt vinegar for apple cider vinegar for a **lighter flavour, adding extra brown sugar for balance.**
Onion Options: Try shallots for a milder onion or mix in a few baby red onions for colour

Storage

Keep sealed jars in a cool, dark place for 2-6 weeks before eating. Flavour improves the longer they mature. Unopened jars last up to 1 year. Once opened, refrigerate and use within 4-6 weeks.

Pickled Red Cabbage
(Traditional Style)

Sharp, sweet, and bold, this pickled cabbage is the perfect companion to a pork pie, ham sandwich, or strong cheddar. Bright pink and a little bossy, it adds tangy punch to burgers, tacos, or salads. The homemade version is worlds apart from supermarket jars of watery purple mush.

Makes: 2 × 500 ml jars (about 1 litre)

Prep Time: 20–30 minutes No cooking (vinegar brine only)

Total Time: 20–30 minutes (plus 24 – 48 hrs pickling)

Ingredients

1 medium red cabbage (about 800g)
1 tablespoon salt (non-iodised, e.g., sea salt or pickling salt)
500ml malt vinegar (or apple cider vinegar for a fruitier note)
150g white granulated sugar (adjust to taste)
1 teaspoon black peppercorns
1 teaspoon mustard seeds
½ teaspoon whole cloves
1 bay leaf or a few juniper berries (optional)

Method

Prepare cabbage.
Remove outer leaves. Quarter, core, and slice cabbage
Finely (2 - 3 mm strips). Place in a large bowl, sprinkle with salt, toss, and leave covered for 6–8 hours or overnight.
Rinse under cold water, drain well, and pat dry with a clean tea towel or use a salad spinner.
Wash jars in hot, soapy water, rinse, then dry in a low oven (120°C) for 10–15 minutes. Boil lids separately for 10 minutes.
Combine vinegar, sugar, and spices in a pan. Heat gently until sugar dissolves, then simmer for a few minutes. Remove from heat. Pack cabbage firmly into warm jars, pressing down as you go. Pour the hot vinegar mixture over the cabbage until it is completely covered. Seal while hot.

Storage

Allow jars to cool, then store in a cool, dark place.
Best left for at least 1 week before eating; the flavour improves after 2–3 weeks.
Unopened jars keep for several months. Once opened, refrigerate and use within 6 weeks.

Special Burger Sauces

Fast-food giants know how to pair sauces with burgers. One balances mild, classic patties, while the other boosts flame-grilled, smoky flavours. Classic Special Sauce pairs well with beef or turkey burgers, while Flame-Grilled Burger Sauce adds depth to chargrilled beef or smoked vegetarian patties.

Makes: Approx 250 g each (enough for 6–8 burgers) **Prep Time:** 10 minutes, no cooking **Total Time:** 10 minutes

Ingredients

120g mayonnaise
2 tablespoons ketchup
1 teaspoon yellow mustard
1 teaspoon sweet pickle relish (or finely chopped pickles; in Australia, try Rosella, Three Threes, or Mrs H. S. Ball's Chutney)
1 teaspoon garlic powder
1 teaspoon onion powder
1 teaspoon white vinegar
½ teaspoon smoked paprika (optional)
Salt and pepper, to taste

Flame-Grilled Burger Sauce

Method

In a small bowl, mix mayonnaise, ketchup, mustard, and relish. Add garlic powder, onion powder, and vinegar, stirring until smooth.
Stir in smoked paprika (if using), and season with salt and pepper. Refrigerate for at least 30 minutes for flavours to develop.

Ingredients

120g mayonnaise
2 tablespoons finely chopped gherkin relish (or sweet pickle relish)
1 tablespoon yellow mustard
1 tablespoon white vinegar
1 teaspoon paprika
1 teaspoon garlic powder
1 teaspoon onion powder
½ teaspoon sugar

Classic Special Sauce

Method

Mix all ingredients in a bowl until well combined. Cover and refrigerate for at least 30 minutes, ideally overnight, to allow flavours to meld.

Storage

Keep both sauces in airtight containers in the fridge for up to 5 days.

More Than Just Veg

"My mum always overcooked the veggies until they were green slime. She's better at it now, she just microwaves them a bit shorter."

— Sorcha MacAonghais

Let's talk about vegetables, especially the ones that make us question our life choices. Brussels sprouts and cabbage could easily win gold at the Boredom Olympics. Nobody dreams of a festive table piled high with them, but every Christmas they show up, as if written into law. Brussels sprouts, those tiny green balls of bitterness often boiled to death, are the culinary equivalent of that one relative who tells the same story on repeat.
Cabbage? The overachiever, always there but never thrilling, even when dressed up with butter and mustard. But here's the secret: with a bit of love (and often a little bacon), even sprouts and cabbage can surprise you.

They might not be the star of the table, but they can stop being the dish everyone politely avoids. Whether roasted with herbs, tossed in a creamy sauce, or finished with a crunchy topping, vegetables can shine.
Roasted root vegetables reveal their natural sweetness, greens take on smoky depth when grilled, and bold spices or a sweet twist can turn boring veg into something worthy of second helpings. This chapter celebrates the ways you can make common vegetables such as Brussels sprouts, carrots, cauliflower, and more sing.
To bring variety to your dinner table, consider creating fresh, light side dishes with clever twists. My classic comforting options will surely please a crowd.

Brussels Sprouts with Walnuts & Blue Cheese
A posh side dish with flair. Broccoli Salad Raw crisp salad with dried fruit, seeds, and a creamy dressing ties into long hot Aussie summers.

Cauliflower Cheese with Crispy Bacon Crumble
Classic with Mum's influence + bacon twist. Comfort and richness.

Mashed Brussels Sprouts with Garlic & Creamy Parmesan
A cheeky take on mash, rich but light.

Roast Butternut Squash & Cumin Soup
Sweet and warming, with subtle citrus highlights. Works well with bread or savoury scones.

Roasted Cauliflower with Lemon, Cumin & Coriander
Warm, aromatic, and bright with herbs and optional paprika.

Sautéed Cabbage with Bacon & Caramelised Onions
School-dinner cabbage redeemed with sweetness and savoury depth.

The Perfect Roasties
Proper roast potato ritual, not deep-fried cheats. Fluffy inside with a crackling crust.

Easy Ways to Take Humble Veg from Sidekick to Showstopper

Roast with Aromatics and Herbs
Carrots roasted with olive oil, honey, salt, and thyme until caramelised.

Sauté with Butter and Fresh Herbs
Green beans tossed in butter with garlic and a squeeze of lemon.

Add a Crunchy Topping
Spinach gratin with a creamy sauce, Parmesan, and breadcrumbs for crisp contrast.

Use Cheese Or Creamy Sauces
Cauliflower cheese with a golden crust from the oven.

Incorporate Spices or Heat
Sweet potatoes roasted with paprika, cumin, and chilli.

Grill for Smokiness
Asparagus grilled with lemon zest and a drizzle of balsamic.

Stuff Vegetables for a Hearty Dish
Zucchini (courgettes) boats filled with quinoa, roasted cherry tomatoes, feta, and herbs.

Add a Sweet Element
Roasted sprouts tossed with pomegranate seeds.

Pickle Or Ferment For Tang
Carrot ribbons quick-pickled with vinegar, sugar, and spice.

Brussels Sprouts
with Walnuts, Blue Cheese & Honey

Brussels sprouts have had a bad press for far too long. Here, they redeem themselves with the crunch of toasted walnuts and the creamy tang of blue cheese. Rich, full of flavour, and just a little bit posh, this side pairs perfectly with roast chicken, beef tenderloin, or even mushroom risotto. And if you fancy it as a meal on its own, well, no one is stopping you. It's proof that sprouts can hold their own without the Christmas table arguments.

Serves: 4 as a side dish
Cook Time: 25 minutes
Total Time: 10 minutes
Prep Time: 10 minutes

Ingredients

500g Brussels sprouts, trimmed and halved
2 tablespoons olive oil
60g walnuts, roughly chopped
50g blue cheese, crumbled
1 tablespoon honey
Sea salt and freshly ground black pepper

Method

Preheat the oven to 200°C. 2. Toss the Brussels sprouts in olive oil, salt, and pepper, then spread on a baking tray. Roast for 20–25 minutes until golden and crispy.
Meanwhile, toast the walnuts in a dry frying pan over medium heat for 3–4 minutes, until fragrant and lightly browned.

Remove sprouts from the oven, drizzle with honey, and top with toasted walnuts and crumbled blue cheese. Serve immediately, allowing the cheese to soften into the warm sprouts.

Tips

Toast the walnuts a day in advance, allow them to cool, and store in an airtight container until ready to use.
Swap walnuts for pecans if you prefer a milder flavour.

Storage & Reheating

Cool completely before refrigerating in an airtight container for up to 2 days. Reheating: Reheat in the oven at 180°C for 10–12 minutes, adding a touch more cheese just before serving to spruce them up.

Mashed Brussels Sprouts
with Garlic & Creamy Parmesan

Brussels sprouts are like the holiday sweater of vegetables—no one wants them, but they always show up anyway. This mashed Brussels sprout dish takes the classic mashed potatoes to the next level with a creamy, cheesy finish and a hint of garlic. Perfect as a rich, indulgent side dish to complement meats or even a vegetarian main course.

Prep Time: 10 minutes
Cook Time: 10-12 minutes
Total Time: 20-22 minutes
Serves: 4 as a side dish

Ingredients

500g Brussels sprouts, trimmed and halved
2 tablespoon butter
3 cloves garlic, minced
120g cream (or milk for a lighter version)
25g of grated Parmesan cheese
Sea salt and freshly ground black pepper
Freshly chopped parsley (optional, for garnish)

Method

Bring a large pan of salted water to the boil and cook the Brussels sprouts for 8-10 minutes until tender. Drain well and return them to the pot.
In a small pan, melt the butter and sauté the garlic for 1 minute, then spoon over the sprouts. Mash until mostly smooth, leaving a few chunks for texture. Stir in the cream and Parmesan until combined, adding a splash more cream if needed. Season to taste with salt and pepper, garnish with parsley (if using), and serve warm.

Tips

Add crispy bacon, sautéed shallots, or lemon zest for extra flavour. Try stirring through some roasted nuts, sun-dried tomatoes, or fresh herbs before serving.

Adaptations & Substitutions

For a dairy-free version, use plant-based alternatives such as butter, cream, and cheese.
Swap Parmesan for Pecorino or Gruyère if you prefer a different cheesy note.

Storage & Reheating

Cool completely before refrigerating in an airtight container for up to 2 days.
Reheating: Reheat gently on the stove with a splash of cream or milk, stirring until hot. Alternatively, microwave in short bursts, stirring between each, until warmed through.

Cauliflower Cheese with Crispy Bacon Crumble

Cauliflower Cheese
with Crispy Bacon Crumble

Mum often made herself cauliflower cheese as a main meal, because she was never much of a meat fan. This version takes that homely favourite and adds a little extra comfort, with a crispy bacon crumble scattered over the top. Golden, crunchy, and rich, it's Cauliflower Cheese the way Mum might have made it if a rasher or two had tempted her.

Serves: 4 as a side dish **Cook Time:** 35 minutes **Total Time:** 50 minutes
Prep Time: 15 minutes

Ingredients

1 large cauliflower, cut into florets
2 tablespoons butter
2 tablespoons plain flour
500ml whole milk
150g cheddar cheese, grated
50g Parmesan, grated
½ teaspoon Dijon mustard
100g cooked bacon, crumbled
Freshly ground black pepper and sea salt

Method

Preheat oven to 200°C and grease a baking dish with butter or spray oil. Boil the cauliflower in salted water for 5-7 minutes, until just tender but not mushy, then drain well.

Meanwhile, melt the butter in a pan, stir in the flour, and cook for 1-2 minutes. Gradually whisk in the milk, stirring until the sauce thickens. If it becomes too thick, add a splash more milk; if it's too thin, simmer for a little longer. Remove from the heat then stir in the cheddar, Parmesan, mustard, salt, and pepper.

Coat the cauliflower with the cheese sauce and transfer it all to the greased dish. Mix the crumbled bacon with the breadcrumbs, then scatter evenly over the top. Bake for 15-20 minutes until golden and bubbling. Serve hot.

Tips

For a crispier topping, use panko breadcrumbs. Make ahead by assembling the dish up to the baking stage, then refrigerate for 24 hours. Bake straight from the fridge, adding 5 minutes to the cooking time.

Serving Suggestions

Serve as a side with roast chicken, beef, or pork, or as a vegetarian main with nut roast. Add a crisp green salad and warm bread to balance the richness of the dish.

Adaptations & Substitutions

For a vegetarian option, replace bacon with crispy fried onions or smoked paprika breadcrumbs. Swap Red Leicester for Gruyère for a lighter, nuttier twist

Storage & Reheating

Cool completely, then cover and refrigerate for up to 3 days. Reheating: Reheat in the oven at 180°C for 20 minutes, or until hot and bubbling. For single portions, microwave gently, adding a splash of milk if the sauce has thickened.

Roasted Butternut Squash & Cumin Soup

For me, pumpkin has long been more of a Halloween prop than an ingredient, carved out and the insides discarded. But butternut squash is the go-to for cooking: sweet, familiar, and versatile, it makes a delicious, warming soup.

Prep Time: 10 minutes
Cook Time: 40 minutes

Total Time: 50 minutes

Serves: 4 as a main meal with bread, toasties, or sides), or 6 as a starter, or light portion.

Ingredients

1.5kg (about 3 lbs) butternut squash, peeled, deseeded, and cut into chunks
2 tablespoons olive oil
1 teaspoon ground cumin
¼ teaspoon ground coriander (optional)
1 large onion, chopped
2 garlic cloves, minced
1 litre (4 cups) vegetable or chicken stock
Salt and pepper, to taste
Splash of cream or a dollop of Greek yoghurt (optional)
Fresh parsley or coriander, to garnish

Method

Preheat the oven to 200°C. Spread the pumpkin on a baking tray, drizzle with one tablespoon olive oil, and sprinkle with cumin, coriander (if using), salt, and pepper. Toss to coat, then roast for 30–40 minutes until soft and golden at the edges.
Meanwhile, heat the remaining oil in a large saucepan over medium heat. Sauté the onion for 5 minutes until softened, then add the garlic and cook for 1 minute more. Stir in the roasted pumpkin and stock, and let it simmer gently for 10 minutes.
Allow to cool slightly, then blend until smooth with a hand blender or food processor. Add extra stock or water if needed to adjust the consistency.
Season to taste, and serve hot, with a swirl of cream or yoghurt and a garnish of fresh herbs.

Tips

For a rustic texture, mash the pumpkin instead of blending. Roast the pumpkin in advance to save time on busy days. Add a knob of butter or extra cream for a richer flavour.

Adaptations & Substitutions

No butternut squash? Sweet potatoes or carrots are good alternatives. **Vegan or dairy-free?** Use coconut milk, oat cream, or cashew cream instead of cream or yoghurt. **Butter substitute.** Olive oil or vegan butter for sautéing.
Cheese substitutes for toppings. Vegan parmesan or cashew parmesan.

Serving Suggestions

Serve with warm, buttered bread, cheese toasties, or savoury scones

Storage & Reheating

Cool completely before storing in airtight containers. Refrigerate for up to 3 days or freeze for up to 3 months.
Reheating from Frozen: Thaw in the fridge overnight before reheating gently on the stove, adding a splash of stock or water if the soup thickens.

The Perfect Roasties

Perfect roast potatoes are the ultimate test of any roast dinner. Nail the roasties, and no one's looking too closely at the sprouts. Anyone can chuck a spud in a fryer, but that's not a roastie, that's a pub snack. The real deal is a ritual: parboil, shake to rough them up, then roast in hot fat until they're shatter-crisp on the outside and cloud-soft in the middle. That's Sunday dinners and Christmas Day on a plate, and no shortcut will ever taste the same.

Prep Time: 15 minutes **Total Time:** 1 hour 15 minutes **Serves:** 4–6 as a side dish
Cook Time: 1 hour

Ingredients

1.5kg Maris Piper potatoes (or any other floury variety; ask your local veg shop for alternatives)
4 tablespoons goose fat, lard, or vegetable shortening (vegan option)
2–3 sprigs fresh rosemary
3–4 garlic cloves, smashed
Sea salt and freshly ground black pepper.
1 teaspoon smoked paprika (optional for a smoky flavour)

Method

Preheat the oven to 220 °C. Peel and cut potatoes into even-sized chunks of approximately 4–5 cm, and place in a large pan of salted water. Boil, then simmer for 10 minutes, or until the edges are tender and soft. Drain in a colander, and shake to rough up the edges for extra crispiness.

Heat goose fat or oil in a roasting tray in the oven for 5 minutes. Add the potatoes to the hot fat, turning to coat evenly. Add rosemary, garlic, salt, pepper, and optional paprika.
Roast for 40–45 minutes, turning halfway, until the outside is golden and crispy.

Tips

Make ahead: Parboil the potatoes the day before, and store them in the fridge.
Extra crispiness: Roughing up the edges after parboiling creates more surface area for crunch. Roast as usual when needed.

Serving Suggestions

Serve immediately alongside roast meats, vegetarian mains, or as part of a hearty Sunday lunch. Perfect for pairing with any roast dinner or festive meal.

Storage & Reheating

Cool completely, then store in an airtight container in the fridge for up to 3 days. You can also freeze roasties for up to 3 months.
Reheating: To reheat, spread the potatoes on a baking tray and roast in a hot oven at 200 °C for 10–15 minutes until crisp again.

Roasted Cauliflower with Lemon, Cumin & Coriander

Roasting cauliflower unlocks its seet, nutty charm, but a hit of lemon, cumin, and coriander (cilantro) elevates it from plain old veg into a warm, aromatic showstopper. Sprinkle on smoked paprika for a cheeky smokiness or scatter fresh parsley for a bright, herby flourish. This dish works just as well for a midweek meal as it does on a party table. Who knew cauliflower could pack this much attitude?

Prep Time: 10 minutes **Total Time:** 40 minutes **Serves:** 4 as a side dish
Cook Time: 30 minutes

Ingredients

1 large cauliflower, cut into florets
3 tablespoons olive oil
1 teaspoon ground cumin
1 teaspoon ground coriander
Zest and juice of 1 lemon
Sea salt and freshly ground black pepper
Fresh cilantro (coriander), chopped, for garnish

Method

Preheat the oven to 200 °C. Toss cauliflower florets with olive oil, cumin, coriander, lemon zest, salt, and pepper.
Spread the florets in a single layer on a baking tray.
Roast for 30–40 minutes, flipping halfway, until golden and tender. Avoid overcrowding to ensure crisp edges.
Drizzle with lemon juice, and garnish with fresh coriander before serving.

Tips

Add ½ teaspoon smoked paprika for a subtle smokiness.
Swap lemon juice for lime for a sharper citrus note. For extra crunch, sprinkle with toasted pine nuts or almonds just before serving.To keep it vegan, avoid yoghurt toppings or use plant-based alternatives.

Serving Suggestions

Perfect alongside grilled chicken, or lamb, or as part of a vegetarian feast.

Storage & Reheating

Cool completely before storing in an airtight container in the fridge for up to 2 days.
Reheating: Reheat in the oven at 180 °C for 10–12 minutes until hot and crisp again.

Sautéed Cabbage with Bacon
& Caramelised Onions

School cabbage earned a reputation, and not a good one. For many of us in Britain, it meant pale, waterlogged leaves ladled out in the dinner hall, smelling faintly of drains and boiled within an inch of their lives. If you didn't have it at school, count yourself lucky; it was less a vegetable and more a childhood trauma on a plate. But with a bit of love and the proper technique, this overlooked vegetable turns into something you'll actually look forward to eating.

Prep Time: 10 minutes
Cook Time: 10 minutes
Total Time: 20 minutes
Serves: 4 as a side dish

Ingredients

1 small head of green cabbage, shredded
2 tablespoons olive oil
4 rashers of bacon, chopped
1 medium onion, thinly sliced
1 tablespoon brown sugar
Sea salt and freshly ground black pepper
Fresh parsley, chopped, for garnish

Method

Heat olive oil in a large frying pan over medium heat. Add the bacon and cook until crispy. Remove and set aside. To the same pan, add the onions and cook over low heat until softened and caramelised, about 15 minutes.
Stir in the shredded cabbage and sprinkle with brown sugar.
Cook until the cabbage is soft and lightly browned, about 10 minutes. Return the crispy bacon to the pan, season with salt and pepper, and stir to combine. Garnish with parsley and serve warm.

Tips

For a vegetarian version, omit the bacon, and add smoked paprika or crispy fried shallots. A splash of apple cider vinegar at the end adds a bright note to the dish. Swap the onions for caramelised shallots for an extra sweet touch.

Serving Suggestions

Pairs beautifully with roast chicken, sausages, or pork. The savoury and slightly sweet flavours balance out hearty mains for a satisfying plate.

Storage & Reheating

Cool completely before refrigerating in an airtight container for up to 2 days.
Reheating: Reheat gently in a frying pan over medium heat until warmed through, or microwave in short bursts, stirring in between.

The Butcher, The Baker
&
The Breakfast Maker

Brekky Burritos

Breakfast has always been an essential part of my life. Growing up, it set the tone not just for the morning, but for how we looked after each other. At the weekend, it wasn't a rushed piece of toast, it was a proper meal to start things off right. Mum was always at the helm of the kitchen, serving up boiled eggs or thickly buttered toast. That rhythm of gathering around the table shaped my love for breakfast as a time that brought us together as a family before heading out into the world.

Dad had his own ritual. On Sundays, he'd take charge with his famous fry-up. Plates piled high, he swivelled the TV around so he could watch the morning news while eating. It was part of the weekend routine, as much a fixture as the bacon on the grill. Sometimes, if we were really lucky, there'd be Rise and Shine on the table, a powdered juice drink that only appeared as a treat.

Simple as it was, it always felt a little bit special.

Weekdays told a different story. We'd race out the door with slices of toast with Marmite in hand, school bags flying, shouting "Bye, Mum!" as we left.

Later, when I owned our first bakery, The Yorkshireman's Pie, I saw breakfast from another angle. By 7 a.m., the tradies were queuing for their cheese and bacon wraps, and most mornings we'd be sold out by 9. It showed me how even a quick bite, grabbed on the run, could still bring comfort.

These days, I catch myself bringing those breakfast moments back to life, hearty bacon and eggs, buttery toast, and even the wraps I once baked at the bakery. Some are old favourites, others more recent additions, but they all carry that same sense of satisfaction.

So, whether you are baking up a storm or frying something golden and crisp, there's a home cooked recipe here for every kind of morning.

Bacon & Egg Sandwich with Tomato Relish & Black Pepper Mayo
Messy, indulgent, and café-style.

Breakfast Pies
Kiwi-inspired, hearty, and perfect for a crowd.

Bubble & Squeak with Garlic Mushrooms
A thrifty British classic revived with garlicky mushrooms.

Home-made British Back Bacon
A step-by-step guide to curing your own..

Irish Potato Farls
Golden wedges of potato bread, simple and comforting.

Kedgeree
Rice, smoked haddock, eggs, and spice for a traditional breakfast dish..

Our Bakery Style Cheese & Bacon Wrap
Puff pastry, molten cheese, and bacon, just like from the bakery counter..

Savoury Pancake Stack with Poached Eggs & Hollandaise
Layered indulgent, and a little theatrical.

Sausage, Bean & Cheese Melt
Flaky Pastry filled with a classic trio.

Brekky Burritos
Soft tortillas wrapped around eggs, bacon, sausage and cheese

Bacon & Egg Sandwich
with Tomato Relish & Black Pepper Mayo

This sandwich takes me back to rainy Sunday mornings when a full fry-up felt like too much effort, but I still wanted something hot, messy, and satisfying. Two-handed and napkin-required, it combines crispy bacon, jammy tomato relish, and black pepper mayo for a café-style indulgence at home.

Prep Time: 10 minutes
Cook Time: 10 minutes
Total Time: 20 minutes
Serves: 2 generously, or 4 smaller portions

Ingredients

Sandwich
2 large slices focaccia (100–120 g each)
4 rashers streaky bacon or 2 rashers back bacon
2 medium-sized eggs
1 tablespoon butter or oil, for frying
Handful of rocket (arugula) or baby spinach (optional)

Tomato Relish (2 tablespoons)
200g cherry tomatoes, halved
1 small red onion, finely chopped
1 tablespoon olive oil
1 tablespoon brown sugar
1 tablespoon red wine vinegar or balsamic vinegar
Pinch of salt
½ teaspoon mustard seeds (optional)

Black Pepper Mayo
3 tablespoons mayonnaise
½ teaspoon freshly cracked black pepper
1 teaspoon lemon juice

Method

Make the Tomato Relish
Heat the oil in a pan, cook the onion until soft.
Add tomatoes, sugar, vinegar, salt, and mustard seeds (if using).
Simmer 15–20 minutes, stirring occasionally, until thickened to a jam-like consistency. Set aside.

Make the Black Pepper Mayo
Mix the mayonnaise, black pepper, and lemon juice.
Taste and adjust the pepper to taste.

Assemble the Sandwich
Cook the bacon until crisp.
Fry eggs to your liking (runny yolks are best).
Lightly toast the focaccia.
Spread the mayo on the bread, then layer the rocket, bacon, egg, and tomato relish.
Top with the remaining focaccia slice and press gently to serve.

Breakfast Pies

Our New Zealand customers often asked us to make these at the bakery, and soon everyone wanted them. Hearty, simple, and comforting, they're baked in small tins for easy portions, perfect for breakfast at home or to share with a crowd.

Prep Time: 15 minutes   **Total Time:** 40 minutes   **Serves:** 6–8 pies
Cook Time: 25 minutes

Ingredients

Pastry
500g plain flour
250g cold butter, cubed
(or 150 g butter + 100 g lard)
Pinch of salt 4–6 tablespoons cold water

Filling
6 large eggs
200g cooked bacon, chopped
1 medium onion, finely chopped
100g cheddar, grated (or a mix with mozzarella)
100g cooked sausage, chopped (optional, use your preferred flavour)
1 small tomato, finely chopped (optional)
40g cooked mushrooms, sliced (optional)
1 tablespoon parsley or thyme, chopped (optional)
Salt and freshly ground pepper

Egg wash
1 egg
1 tablespoon water

Method

Make the Pastry
Rub the butter into the flour and salt until it resembles breadcrumbs. Add water gradually until a dough forms.
Wrap in cling film and chill for 15 minutes.
Preheat oven heat to 180 °C.
Lightly grease 6–8 tart tins or a muffin tray.

Prepare Filling
Whisk eggs in a large bowl.
Add bacon, onion, cheese, and other filling ingredients.
Season with salt and pepper.

Assemble the Pies
Roll out the pastry, line the tins with baking parchment, and fill two-thirds with the mixture.
Cover with the pastry, sealing the edges with water or egg wash.
Cut away the excess pastry and poke steam holes.

Glaze and Bake
Brush tops with egg wash.
Bake 20–25 minutes until golden and set.
Rest 5 minutes before removing from tins.

Storage & Reheating

Cool completely before storing. Keep in an airtight container in the fridge for up to 3 days or freeze for up to 2 months. If freezing, wrap each pie individually for best results.

From fridge: Warm in an oven at 160 °C for 10–15 minutes until piping hot.
From frozen: Bake at 160 °C for 25–30 minutes, loosely covered with foil for the first half, then uncover to crisp the pastry.

Bubble & Squeak
with Garlic Mushrooms

A classic British dish, Bubble and Squeak revives Sunday roast leftovers. Paired with garlicky mushrooms, it makes a warm, comforting dish, perfect for a lazy weekend morning or a cosy start to your day. Simple, satisfying, and nostalgic, it proves that good food doesn't need to be complicated to feel special.

Prep Time: 15 minutes
Cook Time: 15 minutes
Total Time: 30 minutes
Makes: 2 as a main meal

Ingredients

Bubble and Squeak
300 g cooked potatoes (mashed or crushed)
150 g cooked cabbage or Brussels sprouts, finely chopped
1 spring onion or ½ small onion, finely chopped
1 tablespoon butter
1 tablespoon vegetable oil (for frying)
Salt and freshly ground black pepper, to taste

Garlic Mushrooms
250g fresh mushrooms, sliced (button, chestnut, or field)
1 tablespoon olive oil
1 tablespoon butter
2 garlic cloves, finely chopped
1 teaspoon fresh thyme leaves (or ½ teaspoon dried)
A splash of cream or crème fraîche (optional)
Salt and pepper, to taste
Handful of rocket (arugula) or baby spinach, to serve (optional)

Method

Prepare Bubble and Squeak
In a bowl, mix potatoes, cabbage, onion, butter, salt and pepper until combined.
Shape into two rounds or press into one large cake if you prefer.

Cook Bubble and Squeak
Heat oil in a non-stick pan over medium heat.
Fry the rounds for 5–7 minutes per side until golden and crisp. Smaller rounds cook faster.

Cook Mushrooms
Heat the olive oil and the butter in another pan.
Add mushrooms and cook for 5 minutes until they release their moisture and brown.
Add garlic and thyme, cooking for 2 minutes more.
Stir in cream or crème fraîche, (if using), and season with salt and pepper.

Serving Suggestion

Serve bubble and squeak cakes topped with garlicky mushrooms and their pan juices. Add a few rashers of bacon or a fried egg for a full English twist or scatter with rocket (arugula) for a lighter plate.

Storage & Reheating

Cool completely before storing. Keep in an airtight container in the fridge for up to 2 days. Mushrooms are best eaten fresh, but the bubble and squeak cakes reheat well.
Bubble & squeak: Reheat in a lightly oiled frying pan for 4–5 minutes per side until crisp again, or warm through in the oven at 180 °C for 10–12 minutes.
Mushrooms: Warm gently in a pan over low heat, adding a splash of cream or butter to refresh the sauce.

Homemade British Back Bacon

"My husband won't have any other bacon at all now, so it'll be a regular in my house... This is the second go, First one was with shoulder, but definitely better with the loin cut. I bought a cheap little slicer too, which has helped."

-Karen Harkness

If you've lived outside the UK, you know how difficult it is to find authentic British back bacon, unlike streaky bacon, which is mostly fat and crisps quickly. Back bacon balances lean meat and fat for a hearty bite with crisp edges. Cut from pork loin with a thin layer of belly fat, it delivers rich, savoury flavour and firm texture, making it the star of any fry-up or bacon butty. For expats yearning for traditional bacon, making your own from pork loin is surprisingly straightforward and rewarding.

Prep Time: 15 minutes **Total Time:** 30 minutes **Makes:** 2 as a main meal
Cook Time: 15 minutes

Ingredients

1kg pork loin (with a thin layer of fat left on)
50g kosher salt or curing salt mix
25g sugar (white or raw brown)
1 teaspoon black pepper
1 teaspoon ground coriander (optional)
½ teaspoon bicarbonate of soda (optional, helps keep bacon tender)
½ teaspoon nutmeg (optional, for a traditional touch)

Method

Prepare the Pork.
Trim excess fat, leaving a thin 5 mm layer for flavour, then pat the loin dry with kitchen paper.

Apply the cure
Mix all dry ingredients in a bowl. Rub evenly over the pork. Place in a sealable bag.

Cure in the fridge
Store in the coldest part of the fridge for 5–7 days.
Turn daily, massaging juices back into the meat.

Rinse and dry.
Rinse well under cold water, pat dry, and leave uncovered in the fridge for 24 hours to form a slight "skin."

Slice and cook.
Slice thinly for rashers or thicker for bacon chops.
Fry in a dry pan until golden and crisp at the edges.

Adaptions & Substitutions

Curing salt: Prague Powder #1 (pink salt) gives the best colour. If unavailable, use kosher or sea salt (bacon will be paler).
Sugar: Try brown sugar, honey, or maple syrup for deeper flavour.
Cuts: Pork loin is ideal. Tenderloin is leaner; shoulder is fattier and more flavourful.

Irish Potato Farls

Wherever you are along the Irish Sea, the aroma of frying potatoes signals the start of a proper breakfast. In Northern Ireland, farls (soft, flour-dusted wedges of golden potato bread) are griddled until hot and ready to soak up a runny yolk. Cross into Scotland, and the tattie scone takes over: thinner, crisped in butter, often pressed into a roll with bacon or simply spread with butter and jam. Both make thrifty use of leftover mash and are deeply comforting. Best enjoyed at a leisurely pace with a strong cup of tea.

Prep Time: 10–15 minutes
Cook Time: 6–8 minutes
Total Time: 30 minutes
Makes: 4 farls (serves 2–3)

Ingredients

250g cold mashed potato (plain and dry)
50g plain flour, plus extra for dusting
15 g unsalted butter, melted
½ teaspoon salt

Method

Prepare the Mix
Combine mashed potato, melted butter, and salt in a bowl.
Gradually add flour until a soft dough forms.
On a floured surface, pat dough into a round about 1 cm thick.
Cut into four wedges.

Cook the Farls
Heat a dry frying pan over medium heat.
Cook farls for 3–4 minutes per side, until golden brown.
Serve warm with butter, or alongside eggs and bacon as part of a full breakfast.

Scottish Tattie Scones

Prep Time: 10–15 minutes
Cook Time: 6–8 minutes
Makes: 6–8 scones (serves 3–4)
Total Time: About 25 minutes

Ingredients

300 g cold mashed potato (plain and dry)
75g plain flour (plus extra for dusting)
25 g butter
½ teaspoon salt

Method

Mash the butter into the potatoes, then add salt and flour to form a soft dough.
Roll out on a floured surface to 5 mm-thick rounds or triangles.
Fry in a lightly buttered pan for 3–4 minutes per side, until golden.
Serve hot, with a fry-up, butter, or a touch of Marmite.

Tips

Use leftover mash, but avoid mash made with cream or garlic.
To freeze: stack scones with baking paper between each one and freeze raw or cooked. Reheat in a dry pan.

Kedgeree

Kedgeree is a seasoned seafood dish that feels like a warm hug from the past. Once a grand breakfast dish in Britain, it blends rice, smoked fish, eggs, and warming spice into something simple and satisfying. It works just as well for brunch or an easy supper, always with a pot of tea nearby.

Prep Time: 15 minutes
Cook Time: 30 minutes
Total Time: 30 minutes
Serves: 2 as a main dish

Ingredients

300g smoked haddock
200g basmati rice
600ml whole milk
(or half milk, half water)
4 eggs
50g butter
1 small onion, finely chopped
1 teaspoon curry powder
(mild or medium)
½ teaspoon ground turmeric
2 tablespoons chopped parsley or cilantro (coriander), for a fresher twist)
Juice of ½ lemon
Salt and freshly ground black pepper

Method

Cook the Rice Rinse the rice until the water runs clear. Cook in salted boiling water for 10–12 minutes, until just tender.
Drain well and fluff with a fork.

Poach the Haddock
Place the haddock in a shallow pan and cover with milk (or a mix of milk and water). Simmer gently for 5–7 minutes, until the flesh flakes. Remove the fish and reserve the poaching liquid.

Boil the Eggs
Boil the eggs for 8–9 minutes for firm yolks.
Cool in cold water, peel, and quarter.

Make the Flavour Base
Melt the butter in a large pan. Add the onion and cook until soft.
Stir in the curry powder and turmeric, cooking for 1 minute more.

Combine Everything & Serve
Add the rice to the onion mixture with a few spoonfuls of the reserved poaching liquid. Flake the haddock and fold it in gently. Stir through lemon juice, herbs, and season with salt and pepper.
Top with quartered eggs and garnish with parsley.
Add an extra knob of butter on top if you like.

Storage & Reheating

Cool completely before storing. Keep in an airtight container in the fridge for up to 2 days. Because it contains fish and eggs, it's best to eat it fresh and avoid storing it.
To Reheat Reheat gently in a wide pan over low heat, adding a splash of milk, cream, or stock to loosen the rice and prevent it from drying out. Stir often and heat until piping hot. Avoid microwaving if possible, as it can make the fish rubbery and the rice unevenly hot.

Adaptations & Substitutions

Stir in cream for richness. Swap haddock for smoked salmon or trout. Serve with a spoonful of mango chutney on the side.

Our Bakery-Style Cheese & Bacon Wrap

Bacon is great on its own, but combine it with molten cheese and wrap it in puff pastry for pure comfort food. Bake one generous wrap or four petite ones, ideal for sharing, lunchboxes, or a lighter meal.

Prep Time: 5 minutes
Cook Time: 10 minutes

Total Time: 15 minutes

Serves: 1 large wrap or 4 smaller wraps

Ingredients
1 sheet puff pastry, thawed.
2-3 slices raw bacon
2-3 triangles high-melt cheese or cheddar
1 beaten egg, for brushing

Method
Pre-heat oven.
Heat oven to 180 °C and line a tray with baking parchment.
Assemble the Wrap Lay pastry flat in a diamond shape.
For one large wrap, leave whole; for four smaller wraps, cut into four squares.
Place bacon and cheese in the centre. Fold corners over to form parcels, sealing with beaten egg.
Bake
Brush tops with extra egg wash. Bake for 15-20 minutes until puffed and golden.

Adaptations & Substitutions
Add mustard or caramelised onion before folding the pastry.
Australia: Use streaky or shortcut bacon, Mainland or Bega cheddar, Carême or Pampas pastry.
USA: Canadian or thick-cut smoked bacon, sharp cheddar, Pepperidge Farm pastry.
Vegetarian: Replace bacon with smoked tempeh, veggie bacon, or grilled mushrooms.

Storage & Reheating
Storage: Cool completely before storing. Keep in an airtight container in the fridge for up to 3 days or freeze well-wrapped for up to 2 months.
If freezing, separate wraps with baking paper to stop them sticking together.

Reheating: Reheat in a preheated oven at 160 °C for 8-10 minutes until hot and the pastry is crisp again.
From frozen: Bake at 160 °C for 18-20 minutes, loosely covered with foil for the first half, then uncover to allow the top to crisp.

Savoury Pancake Stack
with Poached Eggs & Hollandaise

This recipe started with leftover homemade tortillas. The next morning, our daughter Eva tasted them and said, *"They kind of taste like pancakes."*

Then came her idea: *"Ooh, a pancake stack the size of my face!"* That spark of inspiration led to this layered bake: soft pancakes stacked with spinach, mushrooms, ham, and cheese, baked until bubbling, then topped with poached eggs and hollandaise. Indulgent, a bit theatrical, and entirely Eva's creation.

Prep Time: 15 minutes
Cook Time: 35 minutes
Total Time: 35 minutes
Serves: 4 generous portions (one wedge each, topped with a poached egg)

Ingredients

Pancakes
200g plain flour
2 large eggs
400 ml milk
1 tablespoon melted butter, plus extra for frying
Pinch of salt

Filling
150g baby spinach, wilted and squeezed dry
200g fresh mushrooms, sliced
150g cooked ham or bacon, chopped
150g cheddar or gruyère, grated
2–3 tablespoons crème fraîche
Freshly ground black pepper

Topping
4 medium eggs
150ml hollandaise sauce (homemade or shop-bought)
Fresh parsley or chives, finely chopped

Method

Preheat the oven to 180 °C.
Whisk together the flour, eggs, milk, melted butter, and salt until smooth and then rest the batter for 15 minutes.
Heat a little butter in a non-stick frying pan.
Ladle in enough batter to thinly coat the base and cook for 1–2 minutes per side until golden. Repeat to make 6–8 pancakes for stacking, keeping them warm on a plate as you go.
Wilt the baby spinach in a pan, then squeeze out excess liquid.
Fry the mushrooms until golden.
Chop the ham or bacon into small pieces.

Assemble the stack
Grease a baking dish.
Layer the pancakes with crème fraîche, spinach, mushrooms, ham, and cheese, finishing with a pancake on top.
Spread over a little more crème fraîche and sprinkle with extra cheese. Bake for 15 minutes until golden and bubbling.

Finish and serve
Poach eggs for 3–4 minutes until the whites are set and the yolks remain runny.
Place the eggs on top of the stack, spoon over hollandaise, scatter with herbs, and serve straight away.

Tip
For a reliable shop-bought hollandaise, try Knorr or Maille.
For homemade whisk egg yolks, lemon juice, and melted butter over gentle heat until thickened.

Sausage, Bean & Cheese Melt

Some combinations are iconic: Del Boy and Rodney, tea and biscuits... and sausages, beans, and cheese wrapped in pastry. When sausages, beans, and cheese come together in flaky pastry, it's more than just a snack; it's genuine comfort. This bakery-style melt is flaky, hearty, and quick to make. It's perfect for a satisfying breakfast or a grab-and-go snack.

Prep Time: 10 minutes
Cook Time: 20 minutes

Total Time: 30 minutes

Makes: 6 melts

Ingredients

3 sheets puff pastry, thawed
1 x 400g tin cocktail sausages
1 x 400g tin baked beans (or kidney beans or butter beans if preferred)
250g grated cheese (cheddar, mozzarella or both)
1tsp smoked paprika (or regular paprika)
1 egg beaten (for brushing)

Method

Preheat the oven to 180 °C and line a tray with baking parchment.
Prepare the Filling
Cut the sausages into bite-sized pieces and then mix with the beans, cheese, and paprika in a large bowl.
Prepare the Pastry
Cut each pastry sheet into four squares (12 in total)
Spoon the filling into the centre of each square and then fold pastry over into a triangle or rectangle. Seal edges.
Bake
Place on tray, brush with egg wash, and bake 20–25 minutes until golden and puffed. Serve warm

Adaptations & Substitutions

Sausages: Swap for vegetarian or plant-based options.
Beans: Use chickpeas, lentils, or a bean mix. **Cheese:** Dairy-free alternatives work well. Pastry: Use gluten-free puff pastry.

Storage & Reheating

Cool completely, wrap, and freeze up to 3 months.
To reheat from frozen: Bake at 180 °C for 20–25 minutes, loosely covered with foil, uncovering for the last 5 minutes to crisp.
To reheat from thawed: Bake 10–15 minutes until piping hot.

Brekky Burritos

Breakfast burritos were a bakery standout, selling out quickly each morning. They offer a satisfying and quick breakfast: soft scrambled eggs, crispy bacon, sausage, and melted cheese, all wrapped in a warm tortilla. My friend Denise Lansdown shared this British bakery favourite with me, and it's been part of my mornings ever since.

Prep Time: 15 minutes
Cook Time: 15 minutes
Total Time: 30 minutes
Makes: 2 burritos

Ingredients

- 2 large flour tortillas
- 4 large eggs 4 slices unsmoked back bacon (or any bacon of your choice)
- 2 pork sausages (or flavour of your choice)
- 150g grated cheese
- 2 hash browns
- 2 tablespoons sour cream (optional)
- 1 small tomato, diced (optional)
- A handful of baby spinach (optional)
- 1 teaspoon olive oil or butter, for cooking
- Salt and freshly ground black pepper, to taste

Method

Cook the Meat
Heat a large pan over medium heat.
Cook the bacon and sausages until done, about 5–6 minutes.
Remove and set aside.

Scramble the Eggs
In a bowl, whisk eggs with salt and pepper.
Add oil or butter to the pan, then scramble gently over medium-low heat until just cooked.
Stir in half the cheese until melted.

Warm the Tortillas
Heat tortillas in a dry pan or microwave until pliable.

Assemble the Burritos
Spread sour cream (if using) along the centre of each tortilla.
Add scrambled eggs, bacon, sausages, tomato, spinach, hash brown, and remaining cheese.

Wrap and finish
Fold in the sides, then roll tightly.
Optional: crisp in a hot pan, seam-side down, 1–2 minutes per side.
Slice in half and serve with extra sour cream or hot sauce.

Tips

For a fuss-free bake. Cook the eggs in a greased muffin tin at 180 °C for about 15 minutes, while the sausages, bacon, and hash browns cook alongside.
Add avocado slices or a dash of hot sauce for extra flavour.

Pies & Pastries

There's something undeniably comforting about biting into warm, flaky layers, the golden crust giving way to a rich, savoury filling.
Thanks to Greggs, these little bakes have become an anytime favourite, perfect for a quick lunch on the go or a comforting bite between shopping trips or appointments. For many of us, it's the first place we rush to when touching down in the UK. Because it isn't just about the food, is it? It's the familiar smell, the warmth in your hands on a chilly day, and that first bite that says, you're home.

I can still picture my grandma's kitchen on a cold Sunday morning, the air rich with the smell of something crisping in the oven and sausage sizzling in the pan. She often made a sausage-meat plait, its burnished crust hiding a rich, peppery filling. Looking back, I'm convinced it was the forerunner of today's beloved pork sausage roll, simple, but perfect. Best enjoyed warm from the oven with a generous dollop of brown sauce.

Of course, not every bake goes to plan. Who hasn't popped a tray of something in the oven, only to get distracted and return to a lump of charcoal? That unmistakable smell of "Oops, I've done it again" creeps through the house, followed by frantic waving of a tea towel under the smoke alarm and the reluctant decision that yes, maybe the chippy is the best option tonight. Pastry waits for no one.

The recipes in this chapter aren't just about food, but about memories: packed lunches on school trips, a quick bite on a bustling high street, or something warm shared with family. Whether you're baking from scratch or recreating an old favourite, one thing's sure, there's nothing quite like a proper British bake.
Back home, the bakery cabinets were a treasure trove filled with steak bakes, cheese and onion slices, sausage rolls and pasties, all golden, flaky and impossible to resist.
Walking into a high-street bakery, you never left empty-handed. Abroad, those favourites are almost impossible to find, which is why they've become the recipes so many expats miss the most. This chapter brings them back to life in your own kitchen: from crisp bakery staples to hearty homemade pies, these are the foods that fuelled school lunches, quick teas and Saturday afternoons. And when it comes to another kind of pie, the story gets even better. The football terrace classics deserve a few pages of their own.

Pastry

Cheese & Onion Pasty
Comforting and unmistakably British, crisp, golden pastry filled with savoury cheese, potato and onion.

Chicken Slice
Juicy shredded chicken in a creamy white sauce, wrapped in puff pastry for a proper bakery-style favourite.

The Great British Steak Slice
Tender beef in rich gravy, encased in flaky pastry for the ultimate hand-held bite.

Our Bakery Pork Sausage Roll
Golden, flaky pastry wrapped around seasoned pork sausage meat, a true bakery-counter classic

Our Bakery Pork Pie
The result of years of refinement with a British butcher, made from savoury pork, rich pastry and perfect jelly.

Pork & Egg Pie (Stand Pie)
A traditional pie with a line of hard-boiled eggs through the middle — hearty, nostalgic and made for sharing.

Pie Mash & Liquor
Traditional East End Londonbeefpieswithcreamymash,parsley liquor and chilli vinegar.

Cornish Pasty
Authentic and hearty, with beef, potato,turnip and onion in a sturdy short crust, straight from Cornwall.

Cheese & Onion Slice

Great British Steak Bake

Cheese & Onion Pasty

This homemade take on a bakery classic, which is comforting and unmistakably British, has crisp, golden pastry wrapped around it and a savoury mix of cheese, potato, and onion inside. It's the sort of slice you'd grab from the bakery counter for lunch, or layout on a buffet table. For expats, biting into one brings back memories of quick stops at the high-street bakery, a small but satisfying taste of home.

Prep Time: 20 minutes **Cook Time:** 20-25 minutes **Makes:** 12 slices
Total Time: 40-45 minutes

Ingredients

500g potato flakes, or 3 large potatoes, peeled and boiled
275g frozen chopped onions, or 3 fresh onions, finely chopped
450g mature or extra mature cheddar, grated
20g butter
¼ teaspoon salt
¼ teaspoon pepper
1 pack frozen puff pastry, thawed
1 egg, beaten, for brushing

Method

Boil potatoes until soft, then mash with butter, salt and pepper.
If using potato flakes, prepare as per package instructions and stir in butter, salt and pepper.
Add grated cheese and chopped onions to the mashed potatoes.
Mix well and allow to cool completely.
Cut the pastry into equal rectangles. Place cooled filling on half of the pastry rectangles, then cover with the remaining rectangles.
Press edges together with a fork to seal.
Preheat oven to 180 °C Arrange slices on a baking tray lined with baking paper. Brush with beaten egg and bake for 20-25 minutes until crisp and golden.

Adaptations & Substitutions

Use vintage cheddar for a stronger flavour. Swap mashed potatoes for cream cheese for a Lancashire-style filling.
Pre-made mashed potatoes work for convenience, just adjust seasoning.

Storage & Reheating

Fridge: Cool completely before storing in an airtight container, up to 3 days.
Reheat: Bake at 175 °C for 10 minutes until piping hot and crisp.
Avoid microwaving: It softens the pastry.
Party Tip: Cut the slices smaller before baking, into little squares or fingers, and serve them as warm canapés. They're brilliant with chutneys or dips on a buffet table and always disappear fast.

Serving Suggestion

Serve warm with a fresh green salad or tangy chutney. The crisp pastry and rich filling, paired with something light and sharp, make each bite even more satisfying.

Chicken Slice

These puff pastry parcels, another homemade take on a British bakery classic, contain juicy, shredded chicken in a creamy white sauce. Perfect for a quick lunch, snack or easy dinner, they bring the comfort of bakery food wherever you are. Best of all, you can assemble the bakes ahead of time and refrigerate for up to 24 hours, or freeze for later use, making them a brilliant option for busy home cooks.

Prep Time: 20 minutes
Total Time: 45–50 minutes
Cook Time: 25–30 minutes
Makes: 6 bakes

Ingredients

500ml whole milk (more if needed)
40g unsalted butter
40g plain flour
½ teaspoon salt
2 pinches white pepper
350g cheddar cheese, grated
100g cream cheese
500g chicken breast
1 pack frozen puff pastry, thawed
1 egg, beaten, for brushing

Method

Heat milk, cream cheese and butter in a saucepan until just beginning to boil.

Mix flour with 2 tablespoons cold water to form a slurry.

Stir the slurry and cheddar into the pan, whisking until the mixture thickens. Season with salt and pepper, then remove from the heat and cool completely.

Poach chicken in simmering water for 15 minutes, or until cooked through. Shred while warm, then allow to cool. Stir the shredded chicken into the cooled cheese sauce.

Preheat the oven to 200 °C Cut pastry into equal rectangles. Place half of the rectangles on a lined baking tray.

Spoon 1 heaped tablespoon of filling onto each. Cover with remaining pastry rectangles, pressing the edges together with a fork. Brush the tops with beaten egg. Bake for 20–25 minutes until puffed, golden and crisp. Cool slightly before serving.

Adaptations & Substitutions

Cheese alternative: Use aged Gouda and Parmesan for a sharper flavour.
Dairy-free: Replace whole milk with oat or almond milk and dairy-free cheese.
Pastry swap: Filo with butter or short crust works as an alternative.
Seasoning: Replace white pepper with black, or add a pinch of nutmeg.

To Serve

With coleslaw or baked beans for a classic feel. Pair with chips or salad for a complete meal. Try garlic aioli or buffalo sauce for dipping. Serve with roasted vegetables or sweet potato fries for a modern touch. Fridge: Cool completely, then store up to 3 days. Freezer: Layer with baking paper to prevent sticking; keeps up to 3 months.

Reheat: Bake at 180 °C for 10 minutes (15 minutes if frozen), covered with foil. Uncover for the last 5 minutes to crisp.

The Great British Steak Slice

Enjoy a homemade take on the classic high-street favourite: tender steak and rich, savoury gravy wrapped in buttery, flaky pastry. Perfect for a quick lunch, snack or dinner, these bakes bring all the comfort of the bakery back to your kitchen.

Prep Time: 20 minutes
Total Time: 1 hour
Cook Time: 40 minutes
Makes: 6 bakes

Ingredients

450g rump steak, finely chopped or thinly sliced stir-fry steak
1 onion, diced
1 tablespoon vegetable oil
300ml beef stock (or vegetable stock)
1 tablespoon plain flour
Salt and white pepper, to taste
1 pack frozen puff pastry thawed
1 egg, beaten, for glazing

Method

Cut steak into 1 cm cubes or strips. Heat oil in a frying pan over high heat.
Fry steak until browned. Add onion and cook for 1 minute until softened. Pour in beef stock and bring to the boil. Mix flour with a small amount of water to form a smooth paste, then stir into the beef. Reduce heat, cover, and simmer for 20 minutes, until the gravy has thickened.
Season with salt and pepper. Allow to cool slightly.
Preheat oven to 200 °C. Roll out the puff pastry and cut into squares. Place half on a lined tray. Spoon filling into the centre, leaving a border. Top with the remaining pastry, pressing the edges with a fork to seal. Brush with beaten egg. Bake for 20–25 minutes until the pastry is golden brown and crisp. Cool slightly before serving.

Adaptations & Substitutions

Pastry options: Use shortcrust for a firmer bake, or homemade rough puff. Most supermarkets have their own brands. Here in Australia we have supermarket own or Borgs. Flour for thickening: Cornstarch (US).
Gravy flavour: Add Worcestershire sauce, soy sauce, Bovril, Marmite or Vegemite for extra depth. In North America, Kitchen Bouquet or Gravy Master can serve as substitutes for British gravy browning.

To Serve

Serve hot with chips and peas for a complete meal, or enjoy it straight from the oven as a bakery-style snack. Pair with brown sauce or ketchup for the proper high-street experience.

Storage & Reheating

Fridge: Store cooled bakes in an airtight container for up to 3 days. Freezer: Place baking parchment between layers and freeze for up to 3 months. Reheat: Warm in a 180 °C oven for 15 minutes until hot and crisp. Avoid microwaving the pastry; it goes soft.

Our Bakery Pork Sausage Roll

Flaky, golden and irresistibly savoury, sausage rolls are the star of any British bakery counter. Warm from the oven or served cold at a picnic or Christmas buffet, they're one of those comforting bites that expats struggle to find abroad, where they're often made with beef instead of pork. This homemade take captures the perfect balance of crisp pastry and well-seasoned filling, bringing a proper favourite back to your own kitchen.

When we closed the bakery, one customer told me he still hadn't found a sausage roll quite like ours. Even now, he insists they remain unrivalled.

Prep Time: 15 minutes   **Cook Time:** 20–25 minutes   **Makes:** 12 sausage rolls
Total Time: 35–40 minutes

Ingredients

500g pork sausage meat, or good-quality pork sausages with skins removed
250g breadcrumbs
250ml water
2 teaspoons chives, finely chopped
2 teaspoons parsley, finely chopped
2 tablespoons mustard (English for a sharp kick, Dijon for a milder taste)
½ teaspoon salt
1 teaspoon white pepper
1 pack frozen puff pastry, thawed
1 egg, beaten, for brushing

Tips

Use a piping bag to distribute sausage meat neatly. Cut with a pizza cutter or bench scraper for clean edges. Add cranberry sauce to the filling at Christmas.

Method

In a bowl, combine breadcrumbs, water, salt, pepper, chives and parsley. Add sausage meat and mustard, mixing thoroughly by hand until well combined.

Preheat oven to 200 °C. Place the puff pastry on a floured surface. Place the sausage mixture in a log along one edge of the pastry. Brush the opposite edge with beaten egg, roll the pastry over the filling, and seal with the egg-washed edge. Place seam-side down. Cut into 12 equal pieces for party-sized rolls, or into 4–6 larger portions if you prefer. Place on a baking tray lined with baking paper. Brush the tops with beaten egg and bake for 20–25 minutes, until golden and crisp. Cool slightly before serving.

Adaptations & Substitutions

Abroad: If British sausages aren't available, use mild pork. Remove the casings before use.
Shortcuts: Substitute breadcrumbs with a box of sage and onion stuffing mix, then combine with sausage meat.
Pastry sourcing: Frozen puff pastry is often available in international food shops or in the freezer section of supermarkets.

To Serve

Classic style: Warm with HP sauce or English mustard. Buffet spread: Pair with pickles, cheese cubes and grapes. Pub meal: Add chunky chips and coleslaw or baked beans.

Storage & Reheating

Fridge: Store in an airtight container for up to 3 days. Freezer: Freeze baked rolls for up to 3 months. Reheat: Bake at 180 °C for 5–10 minutes until piping hot. Microwaving works in a pinch but softens the pastry.

Our Bakery Pork Pie

Steve, my trusted British butcher, and I spent three years perfecting a pork pie that stood out. We refined every detail, from the meat to the pastry, to find the perfect balance: savoury pork, rich crust, and just the right amount of jelly.
We began creating our version of the renowned Melton Mowbray, the pork pie that sets the standard. Not to copy, but to match its quality. The aim was a modern pork pie that still felt distinctly British. After years of testing and tasting, we finally created a pie with its own personality. Bold, balanced, and full of care, it quickly became a customer favourite at the bakery.

Prep Time: 30-40 minutes
Cook Time: 40-50 minutes
Total Time: 1 hour 10-30 minutes
Makes: 8 large pies or 10 small pies

Ingredients

Hot Water Crust Pastry
700g plain flour, plus extra for rolling
2 teaspoons salt
110 g lard
10 g butter (or all lard)
280ml water

Filling
2kg pork shoulder, diced
600g unsmoked British gammon or diced bacon
2 tsp fresh sage, chopped
2 teaspoons salt
2 teaspoons nutmeg
2 teaspoons white pepper

Jelly
1 litre water
1 chicken stock cube
1 bay leaf
1 sprig thyme
1 sage leaf (or ½ teaspoon dried)
½ onion, halved
½ carrot, chopped
½ celery stick with leaves 10 black peppercorns
Gelatine, (approx. 2 teaspoons per 500ml)

Method

Preheat oven to 180 °C Sift flour and salt into a bowl. Heat lard, butter and water in a pan until melted and just boiling. Pour liquid into the flour, stirring quickly with a spoon. Knead lightly until smooth.
Cover with clingwrap and rest 10-15 minutes.
Mix salt, nutmeg, pepper and sage. Toss through the pork and gammon until evenly coated. Roll out the pastry and line greased pie tins (10 cm for large, 7 cm for small). Firmly pack with the pork filling.
Add pastry lids, sealing edges tightly, and cut a steam hole in the centre.
Bake small pies for 30 minutes or large pies for 50 minutes, until the filling reaches an internal temperature of 70 °C .
Remove from tins if you desire, brush sides with beaten egg, and return to the oven for 10 minutes. Cool for 20 minutes.
Simmer water, stock cube, herbs, vegetables and peppercorns for 5 minutes. Strain. Dissolve gelatine in a little hot stock, then stir back in. Cool until just warm. Using a funnel or syringe, pour the jelly slowly into the steam hole. Let it settle, then top up as needed. Chill overnight for the jelly to set.

Storage
Store in an airtight container in the fridge for 3-7 days.

Tips
Butter in the crust: Adds flavour, moisture and a golden colour. It makes the pastry easier to handle while keeping it sturdy.
Prepare jelly first: Make it while the pies bake, so it's cooled and ready to pour once the pies have rested.

Pork & Egg Pie (Stand Pie)

Whether you picked out the egg as a child or savoured every bite, this homemade version delivers all the flavours of a proper butcher's pork and egg pie. A true British classic, the Pork & Egg (or Stand Pie) takes centre stage at any picnic, buffet or gathering. The golden hot water crust, seasoned pork filling and signature line of eggs through the middle make for a hearty, nostalgic slice. Serve cold with a dollop of pickles, or enjoy as part of a meal with apple slaw, a fresh green salad or even Coronation Chicken on the side. A crisp cider or a glass of Pimm's pairs beautifully with the rich flavours of the pie.

Prep Time: 30 minutes
Cooling Time: At least 2 hours
Cook Time: 1 hour 15 minutes
Total Time: Approx 4.5 hrs includes chilling
Makes: 1 pie in a 20 cm round tin or 1 pie in a 23 cm loaf tin

Ingredients

Hot Water Crust Pastry
700g plain flour, plus extra for rolling
2 teaspoon salt
110g lard
110g butter (or all lard)
280 ml water

Filling
2kg pork shoulder, diced
600g unsmoked gammon or diced bacon
2 teaspoons fresh sage, chopped
2 teaspoons salt
2 teaspoons nutmeg
2 teaspoons white pepper

Jelly
1 litre water
1 chicken stock cube
1 bay leaf
1 sprig thyme
1 sage leaf (or ½ teaspoon dried)
½ onion, halved
½ carrot, chopped
½ celery stick with leaves
10 black peppercorns
Approx. 2 tsp gelatine

To Assemble - 5 hard-boiled eggs peeled, 1 egg beaten for glazing

Method

Melt lard, butter and water in a pan until just simmering. Stir in salt. Pour flour into the bowl and mix to form a rough dough. Knead lightly until smooth, adding a drop of water if too dry. Wrap in clingfilm and chill for 30 minutes.

Mix pork shoulder, gammon, sage, nutmeg, salt and pepper until evenly combined. Preheat oven to 180 °C Roll out two-thirds of the pastry and line a greased 20 cm pie tin (springform tin for easier release) or 23 cm loaf tin, pressing firmly into the sides. Place some of the mixture on the base of the pie, then arrange hard-boiled eggs in a line down the centre. Encase the eggs in the pork mixture, pressing gently but firmly into place.

Roll out the remaining pastry for a lid, place on top, seal edges and cut a steam hole. Brush with beaten egg. Bake for 1 hour 15 minutes, until golden and the filling reaches an internal temperature of 70 °C.

Cool completely in the tin before unmoulding.

If needed, loosen edges with a knife. Simmer water, stock cube, herbs, vegetables and peppercorns for 5 minutes. Strain and taste for desired seasoning.

Once the stock is ready, pour a little into a measuring jug and dissolve the gelatine in it. Stir until smooth, then top up with stock to make 500 ml in total. Cool until just warm. Using a funnel or syringe, trickle jelly into the steam hole a little at a time, letting it settle before topping up. Chill overnight to set.

Storage & Reheating

Fridge: Store in an airtight container for up to 3 days. Freezer: Wrap tightly and freeze for up to 1 month. Thaw in the fridge before serving (Note: freezing may slightly affect the look of the eggs).

Pie, Mash & Liquor
Traditional Cockney Style

Soft, flaky pastry with a hearty minced beef filling, served with creamy mash and a ladle of parsley sauce, or " liquor."

A true East End classic, pie, mash and liquor began as humble street food for London's workers in the 1800s and became a staple of family-run pie shops across the city. For expats, making it at home brings back all the comfort and nostalgia, no eels required.

Prep Time: 40 minutes (plus 30 minutes chilling) **Total Time:** At least 2 hours **Serves:** 4
Cook Time: 1 hour 20 minutes

Ingredients

Pastry
250 g plain flour
125 g shredded suet
Pinch of salt
150 ml cold water

Filling
500 g minced beef
1 medium onion, finely chopped
2 tablespoon plain flour
250 ml beef stock
1 Tbsp Worcestershire sauce
Salt and black pepper to taste

Mash
1kg floury potatoes
75g butter 100 ml milk Salt and white pepper

Liquor
30g butter
30g plain flour
500 ml fish stock (or vegetable stock, or half vegetable, half chicken stock)
Salt and black pepper, to taste
Handful of fresh parsley, finely chopped
Pinch of salt

Chilli Vinegar
500 ml white wine vinegar (or malt vinegar for a more pungent taste)
4-6 fresh red chillies, sliced lengthwise, seeds removed
2 garlic cloves, lightly crushed (optional)

Quick Version
250 ml white wine vinegar (or malt vinegar)
2 red chillies, finely sliced
1 garlic clove, lightly crushed

Method

Mix flour, suet and salt. Add enough cold water to form a soft dough. Wrap in clingfilm and chill for 30 minutes.
Fry onion until soft, then add mince and cook until browned. Stir in flour, then add stock and Worcestershire sauce.
Simmer for 15 minutes until thickened. Allow to cool (room temp)

Preheat oven to 200 °C Roll out two-thirds of the pastry to line 4 individual greased pie tins. Spoon the cooled filling.
Roll out the remaining pastry, cut lids and seal the edges.
Prick tops to allow steam to escape. Bake for 35-40 minutes until golden.
Boil potatoes until tender. Drain and mash with butter, milk and salt and pepper until smooth.

The Liquor
Melt butter in a pan, then stir in flour to make a roux. Gradually whisk in hot stock.
Simmer for 5 minutes until smooth and slightly thickened. Stir in parsley and season with a pinch of salt.

Pie, Mash & Liquor

Prepare the Chilli Vinegar

Infused: Using a sterilised bottle, add vinegar, chillies and garlic if using. Seal and leave in a cool, dark cupboard for 1 week. Strain if preferred, or leave the chillies in.
Quick: Warm vinegar gently (do not boil). Add chillies and garlic and steep for 10–15 minutes. Pour into a bottle and serve immediately.

To Serve

One pie per person with generous scoops of mash. Ladle liquor over the top, and add a splash of chilli vinegar for the proper East End experience.

Tips

Many supermarkets sell pre- mixed suet, which works perfectly in the pastry. For authenticity, serve with two ice cream scoops of mash, not just any old dollop. Resist the temptation to add gin because traditionally liquor is parsley-based, not alcoholic!

Cornish Pasty

Cornish pasties are pure comfort food. Just a whiff takes me back to childhood holidays in Perranporth with its briny sea air, my sandy toes and a steaming pasty in hand. Nothing beats it.

Prep Time: 30 minutes (plus 3 hrs chilling)
Cook Time: 40 minutes
Total Time: About 1 hour 10 minutes (plus chilling)
Makes: 6-8 pasties

Ingredients

Pastry
600g strong bread flour (bread flour)
100g chilled unsalted butter
100g lard (or vegetable shortening/all-butter for vegetarian)
Pinch of salt
6 tablespoons cold water

Filling
1 onion, finely chopped
2 potatoes, diced 1 swede (or turnip), diced
350g beef skirt or chuck steak, finely chopped
Salt and pepper, to taste
2 tablespoons of butter
1 egg beaten, for glazing

Method

Rub butter and lard into flour and salt with your fingertips (or pulse in a food processor) until it resembles fine breadcrumbs.
Gradually add water to form a firm dough.
Divide into 4 portions, wrap in clingfilm and chill for at least 3 hours (overnight is best). Chilling the dough makes it easier to handle and results in a firmer, flakier crust.
Preheat oven to 220 °C. Mix onion, potato, swede, beef, salt and pepper.
Roll out each portion of chilled dough on a floured surface into a 23 cm round, about 5 mm thick. Use a plate as a template if helpful.
Place a quarter of the filling in the centre of each round, leaving 1" border. Add a pat of butter on top. Brush edges with egg.
Fold pastry over into a half-moon and crimp the edges firmly to seal. Transfer to a lined baking tray. Brush tops with egg and cut 2 small slits in each pasty.
Bake for 40 minutes until golden and crisp. Cool slightly before serving.

Storage & Reheating

Fridge: Store cooled pasties in an airtight container for up to 3 days.
Freezer: Wrap individually with clingfilm, then foil-wrap, and freeze for up to 3 months. Thaw overnight in the fridge.
Reheat: Place on a tray, cover with foil, and bake at 180 °C for 15-20 minutes until hot.

Tips

Great pastry matters: Strong, bakers flour makes a firmer, traditional crust. Layer carefully: Onion first, then potato, then swede, and finally meat on top.
This helps prevent the raw vegetables from breaking through the pastry.
Keep it juicy: Adding little pats of butter ensures the filling stays moist.
Swede or turnip: Purists say swede, but turnip adds a tasty twist.
Plan ahead: The pastry benefits from an overnight chill in the fridge.

Football, Pies & Expat Life
A British Tradition

The air outside a stadium has its own magic: the hum of chatter, scarves pulled tight against the cold, and the unmistakable smell of hot pies. Standing shoulder to shoulder in the crowd, steam rising from meat pie in hand, you're instantly transported back to a home match in Britain.

When living abroad, the match day ritual stays the same. Whether you call it soccer or footy, supporters need a pie in hand. In Australia, you'll find decent substitutes such as the Pie Shop in Melbourne, the Great Aussie Pie in Sydney, or the trusty Four N Twenty when the craving strikes. They'll keep the spirit alive, but nothing quite replaces the British versions we grew up with.

Football traditions travel with us. Expat pubs stream the games, viewers' accents mingle over pints, and for ninety minutes, you could almost be back home in England.
Or you can recreate the atmosphere yourself: scarf on, pint poured, pie in the oven, turning your living room into a terrace of its own.

Everyone has their match-day favourite- a Killie Pie in Scotland, a Balti Pie further south, mushy peas with a minced beef pie, all washed down with a pint.
Pies belong to football as much as the chants, the cold air, and the sense of belonging in the stands. That's why this book includes Britain's best-loved footie pies, so you can bring the flavours of the terraces into your own kitchen, wherever you are.
A hot pie and the roar of the match, that's what keeps the feeling of home alive.

A Little Surprise for the Hubs

Want to earn serious brownie points? Next time his team's on, surprise your other half with a homemade footie pie. Pop a Killie Pie in the oven, serve it with mushy peas or chips, and hand him a cold pint (or a cuppa if it's an early kick-off). It's an insignificant gesture that says, I see you, and yes, I love you enough to make you a pie for the game. Trust me, it'll go down a treat, and you might even get control of the remote after the final whistle.

Footie Pies

Traditional Scotch Pie
The original footie pie, with a peppery lamb or mutton filling in golden hot water crust, a staple across Scottish football grounds.

Killie Pie
A warm, meaty Scottish steak pie inspired by the famous Killie Pie

Chicken Balti Pie
Bold and aromatic curry filling wrapped in pastry, a Lancashire and Yorkshire match-day favourite since the 70s and 80s.

Peppery Minced Beef Pie (Cardiff City Favourite)
Inspired by Cardiff's famous Clarkie's pies, peppery minced beef in a sturdy crust, built for eating on the go

Balti Chicken Pie

Traditional Scotch Pies

Often called the original footie pie, the Scotch pie has been a match-day favourite in Scotland for decades. With its peppery lamb (or mutton) filling and golden hot water crust, this sturdy little pie is a true Scottish icon. Whether bought from a bakery, eaten at the football or pulled from the fridge the next day, it never disappoints. Traditionally served with baked beans or mash, sometimes perched on top of both, Scotch pies have long been part of chip shop counters, school dinners and family tables. Simple, satisfying and full of flavour, they're proof that once you've made them from scratch, you'll never look back. Hot or cold, with or without brown sauce, one thing's certain: you can't stop at just one.

Prep Time: 1 hour 30 minutes
Cook Time: 35–40 minutes
Total Time: Approx. 2 hours 15 minutes
Makes: 6 small pies (10 cm tins or rings)

Ingredients

Hot Water Crust Pastry
100g lard (or beef dripping for authentic flavour)
100ml water
250g plain flour
½ teaspoon salt
1 beaten egg (for sealing and glazing)

Meat Filling
400g minced lamb (or beef if preferred)
1 small onion, finely chopped or grated
1 teaspoon salt
½ teaspoon ground white pepper
½ teaspoon ground black pepper
¼ teaspoon ground nutmeg (optional but traditional)
2 tablespoons beef stock or water

Method

Preheat oven to 180 °C. Mix the mince, onion, seasonings and stock in a bowl until combined. Cover with clingfilm and refrigerate until needed. The mixture should feel soft but not wet.
Gently heat the lard and water in a pan until melted and just bubbling. Combine flour and salt in a bowl, pour in the hot liquid, and stir into a dough. Cool slightly, then knead until smooth. While still warm, divide into 6 pieces.
Use two-thirds of each dough piece to line greased pie tins or rings (8–10 cm). Roll the pastry to approx 5mm thickness, line the tins and then press pastry up the sides evenly. Patch cracks if needed. Spoon in filling, pressing lightly but not too firmly. Roll out the remaining dough for lids, place on top and seal edges. Cut a steam hole in the centre and brush with egg.
Bake for 35–40 minutes until golden and cooked through.
Rest 5–10 minutes before serving.

Storage & Reheating

Fridge: Wrap individually in clingfilm and store up to 3 days.
Freezer: Wrap individually in clingfilm and freeze up to 2 months. Thaw in the fridge overnight. Reheat: Bake at 180 °C for 15–20 minutes until hot and crisp. **Serving Suggestions:** Warm or cold, with brown sauce or baked beans. For a chip shop feel, serve with mash, mushy peas or chips.

Adaptations & Substitutions

Meat: Use lamb or mutton if available. Otherwise, mix beef and pork mince for extra depth. Add nutmeg or allspice for that butcher's shop flavour.
Fat: You can also substitute suet with grated butter, lard, or vegetable shortening.
Extra flavour: A spoon of Worcestershire sauce or beef stock concent' boosts richness.

Killie Pie
Scottish Steak Pie

Want to impress your partner during the game? Dish up a homemade Killie Pie with mushy peas or chips, and a drink on the side. It's a move that could score you more points than the team on screen. This steak pie became a match-day favourite at Rugby Park in the 1990s, and it's still a fan favourite today. Warm, meaty, and wrapped in pastry, it's the pie that makes wintry nights bearable and TV football that much better.

Prep Time: 30 minutes (plus 30 minutes chilling)
Cook Time: 1 hour

Makes: 4 individual pies or 1 large pie
Total Time: 1 hour 30 minutes

Ingredients

Pastry
250g plain flour
125g cold unsalted butter (or half butter, half lard for a crisper finish), diced
Pinch of salt
2–3 tablespoons cold water
250g puff pastry (for the top) — ready-made works fine
1 beaten egg, for glazing

Filling
500g stewing or chuck steak, diced
1 tablespoon plain flour
Salt and black pepper
1 tablespoon vegetable oil
1 onion, finely chopped
2 garlic cloves, minced
300ml beef stock (use Oxo, Bovril, or another rich cube)
1 teaspoon Worcestershire sauce (or Marmite/Vegemite for depth)
1 teaspoon tomato paste (optional, for richness)

Method

Preheat oven to 200 °C. Put flour and salt in a large bowl.
Rub in butter with your fingertips until the mixture looks like fine breadcrumbs (or pulse in a food processor).
Gradually add cold water, 1 tablespoon at a time, mixing with a knife until the dough comes together. Gather into a ball, wrap in clingfilm, and chill in the fridge for at least 30 minutes.
Toss diced steak with flour, salt, and pepper. Heat oil in a pan, brown the meat in batches, and then set aside. In the same pan, cook onion and garlic until soft. Return the meat to the pan. Add stock, Worcestershire sauce, and tomato paste. Simmer gently for 1½ to 2 hours, until the meat is tender and the gravy has thickened.
Cool completely.
Roll out the shortcrust pastry to approx. 5mm and line greased tins or a pie dish. Blind-bake the bases with parchment paper and baking beans if you want to avoid soggy bottoms, then cool. Spoon the cooled filling.
Roll out puff pastry for the lids, place them on top, seal, and crimp the edges with a fork. Cut a small steam hole in the pie lid and brush with beaten egg.
Bake pies for 25–30 minutes until golden and puffed.

Tips

No Oxo? Use gravy granules, or dissolve a teaspoon of Vegemite in water for beefy depth. In Australia, most supermarkets sell ready-made pastry that works well.

Serving Suggestions

Serve hot with mushy peas or chips for a proper match-day plate. Add a splash of brown sauce (HP or homemade) to rekindle the full terrace experience.

Chicken Balti Pie

Balti pie is a true match-day favourite, especially at football grounds in Lancashire and Yorkshire, where curry pies first became popular in the 1970s and 80s. Packed with bold, aromatic flavours, it's a perfect way to bring curry night and footie night together.

Prep Time: 30 minutes (plus 30 minutes chilling)
Total Time: 1 hour 30 minutes
Total Time: 1 hour 30 minutes
Cook Time: 30 minutes

Ingredients

Pastry
200g plain flour 100 g fat (50g butter + 50g lard, or 100g all-butter, or 100g vegetable shortening) ¼ teaspoon salt
4–5 tablespoons cold water

Filling
30g oil
500g chicken breast, diced (or use chickpeas, paneer, or tofu for a vegetarian option)
1 medium onion, chopped
2 garlic cloves, crushed
1 tablespoon tomato paste
1½ tablespoons plain flour
120ml chicken stock
2 tablespoons balti paste (see homemade option below)
1 × 400g tin chopped tomatoes
100g frozen peas

To Finish
1 sheet puff pastry
1 large egg, lightly beaten

Method

Preheat oven to 180 °C. Mix flour, fat, and salt until the mixture resembles breadcrumbs. Add cold water gradually until the dough comes together. Wrap in cling wrap and chill in the fridge for 30 minutes.
Heat oil in a pan. Brown the chicken in batches, then set aside.
Add onion and garlic to the pan, cooking until soft. Stir in tomato paste and Balti paste, cook for 2–3 minutes. Add flour, stir for 1 minute, then gradually add the stock. Add tinned tomatoes and peas, and simmer for 10–15 minutes, until the sauce thickens and the chicken cooks through. Cool slightly.
Roll out the shortcrust pastry to about 3–4 mm thick. Line individual 10 cm pie tins or one large pie dish. Fill with cooled mixture. Top with puff pastry, trim the edges, seal well with a fork, and brush with beaten egg. Bake for 25–30 minutes until golden and crisp.

Serving Suggestions

Add cucumber raita or tamarind chutney for freshness. Pair with spiced potato wedges or cumin rice for a heartier meal. A cold lager or ginger ale makes this the perfect match.

Tips

Store cooled leftovers in the fridge for up to 3 days.
Reheat at 160 °C for 10–15 minutes. Freeze baked pies (well wrapped) for up to 2 months. Reheat from frozen at 160 °C for 25–30 minutes.

Homemade Balti Paste (quick blend)
1 teaspoon turmeric
1 teaspoon paprika
1 teaspoon ground coriander
½ teaspoon cumin seeds
¼ teaspoon ground cinnamon
1 cm ginger, peeled and chopped
1 garlic clove
¼–½ teaspoon chilli powder, to taste
1–2 teaspoons oil

Peppery Minced Beef Pie
A Cardiff City Favourite

A proper match-day legend from Cardiff, this pie is all about practicality and flavour. The pie's peppery minced beef filling and thick pastry allowed for eating on the go. No plate needed, just a pie in hand and the roar of the crowd. For Cardiff expats, it's pure nostalgia, a direct link to home and the spectator terraces of Ninian Park.

Inspired by the famous peppery Clarkie's beef pies of Cardiff, these hearty hand-held bakes have a thick crust and a no-nonsense filling, designed to satisfy and transport you straight back to match day.

Prep Time: 30 minutes (plus 30 minutes chilling)
Cook Time: 25–30 minutes
Makes: 6 pies
Total Time: About 1 hour 15 minutes

Ingredients

Pastry
- 350g plain flour
- 175g lard or butter (or a mix of both)
- Pinch of salt
- 4–5 tablespoons cold water

Filling
- 500g beef mince
- 2 medium onions, peeled, finely chopped
- 1 tablespoon plain flour
- 250ml beef stock
- 1 teaspoon Worcestershire sauce
- ½ teaspoon ground white pepper (more for the authentic Cardiff kick)
- Salt, to taste
- 2 medium onions, peeled, finely chopped
- 1 tablespoon plain flour
- 250 ml beef stock
- 1 teaspoon Worcestershire sauce
- ½ teaspoon ground white pepper (more for the authentic Cardiff kick)
- Salt, to taste
- 1 beaten egg, for glazing

Method

Preheat oven to 200 °C. Rub the fat into the flour and salt until it resembles breadcrumbs. Add cold water, a spoonful at a time, until the dough comes together. Wrap in clingfilm and chill in the fridge for 30 minutes.

Fry onions until softened. Add mince and cook until browned. Sprinkle over the flour, stir well, then add the stock, Worcestershire sauce, white pepper, and salt. Simmer for 15–20 minutes until thick. Cool completely.

Roll out the pastry to 5mm and cut into circles large enough to line greased pie tins with some overhang. Fill with the cooled beef mixture. Cover with pastry lids, crimp the edges with a fork to seal, and cut a small steam hole. Brush with beaten egg.

Bake for 25–30 minutes until the pastry is firm, golden, and crisp.

Adaptations & Substitutions

You can swap the minced beef for minced lamb for a softer, richer filling. A little extra white pepper gives the classic Cardiff bite. If you prefer a thicker crust, roll the pastry slightly heavier and bake until firm and deep golden. A spoon of finely chopped pickled onion or a dash more Worcestershire sauce adds a livelier edge without changing the character of the pie.

Storage & Reheating

Let the pies cool fully, then keep them in an airtight container in the fridge for up to three days. They reheat well in a moderate oven until the pastry is crisp again. They also freeze neatly once baked. Wrap each pie and store for up to three months. Defrost in the fridge and warm through in the oven.

Picnics & Sandwiches

Here's a wild, crazy confession...
I hated making school lunches for the kids; sandwiches were the bane of my life. My children would beg for a certain filling one week, then flatly refuse it the next, leaving me with lunchboxes that came home exactly as they went out. In desperation, I swapped the bread for carrot sticks, hummus, cheese cubes, and fruit. Those saintly little options made me feel virtuous, but I was secretly envious of mums who just threw in a packet of crisps, packaged cheese and crackers and yoghurt pouches. Somehow, we parents all keep at it, sneaking in treats or clever swaps just to make sure something from the lunchbox gets eaten.
Anyone who's ever made their own sandwiches knows why UK supermarket ready-made fillers like cheese and onion, egg mayo, or chicken mayo with sweetcorn are so beloved. They're cheap, cheerful, and above all convenient.
Unlike the super-organised parents who prepped the night before, I was usually rummaging in the fridge half an hour before school, trying to find a slice of Billy Bear ham while refereeing the morning chaos. Come 8:30am, I'd be wrestling with butter that was too cold (tearing the bread). Bread that was too fresh (falling apart) and marmite that was too sticky (causing a meltdown).

And let's not even talk about Instagram-perfect lunchboxes, filled with colourful, nutritionally dense, perfectly packed snacks. My biggest concern? Making sure I didn't forget to actually put the lunchboxes in the school bags.
This chapter offers the solution for those of us dreading daily sandwich duty. These delicious supermarket-style sandwich fillers will ensure your lunchboxes come home empty.

You'll find simple, reliable recipes and tips taking the guesswork out of packed lunches. They help you save time, cut down on waste, and skip the early-morning meltdowns, not to mention the grim task of digging out untouched lunchboxes from the bottom of school bags.
I hope your favourite Tesco-style sandwich filler has made it into the pages of this chapter. And a high-five to you, fellow sandwich makers, and to every parent for whatever you manage to pack into those school bags.

Sandwiches & Picnics

Croque Monsieur
The posh toastie, bechamel and all, straight out of Paris.

Reuben Toastie
A deli classic, stacked with pastrami, cheese, and tangy sauerkraut.

Tandoori Chicken Sandwich
Smoky chicken, spiced mayo, and mango chutney, an Indian-inspired favourite.

Cheese & Onion Quiche
A timeless bake, crisp pastry with endless filling options.

Scotch Eggs
The Yorkshireman's Pie, our bakery favourite, crisp on the outside, rich and hearty inside.

Chicken Shawarma Sandwich
Juicy spiced chicken grab and go lunch

Croque Monsieur

If a toastie went to finishing school in Paris, this would be the result. The Croque Monsieur is no ordinary ham and cheese; it's ham and cheese on holiday, lounging under a blanket of bechamel, with a golden crust that says, "Ooh la la."

Makes: 2 sandwiches
Prep Time: 10 minutes
Cook Time: 10 minutes
Total Time: 20 minutes

Ingredients

For the sandwich
4 slices white bread
2 tablespoons butter, softened
2 teaspoons Dijon mustard
100g sliced ham
100g Gruyère cheese, grated (or Emmental)
200ml bechamel sauce (see below)

For the Bechamel Sauce
15g butter
15g plain flour
200ml milk
Pinch nutmeg Salt and black pepper, to taste

Method

Melt butter in a saucepan, then stir in flour and cook for 1 minute. Gradually whisk in milk until smooth and thickened. Season with nutmeg, salt, and black pepper. Butter one side of each slice of bread. Spread Dijon mustard on the other side of two slices. Place the ham and half the cheese on the mustard sides, then top with the remaining bread, butter-side out.
Fry or toast until golden brown and the cheese inside is melting. Transfer to a baking tray, spoon the béchamel over the tops, and scatter with the remaining cheese. Grill for 3-4minutes until bubbling and golden.

Adaptations & Substitutions

Croque Madame: Add a fried egg on top for the traditional variation.
Cheese Swap: Use cheddar or mozzarella if Gruyère isn't available.
Quick Version: Skip the bechamel and just add extra cheese before grilling.

Storage

Best eaten fresh. If needed, store in the fridge for 1 day and reheat under the grill.

Reuben Toastie

The Reuben is so popular here in Western Australia I'm half convinced there's a secret society devoted to it. Somewhere out there, a group of sandwich lovers are meeting in dark corners, raising a toastie in honour of corned beef, sauerkraut, and way too much cheese.

Makes: 2 sandwiches

Prep Time: 10 minutes

Cook Time: 5–6 minutes

Total Time: Approx 10–12 minutes

Ingredients

4 slices Rye bread
2 tablespoons butter, softened
2 tablespoons Russian dressing (or Thousand Island)
4 slices Swiss cheese
150g sliced corned beef or pastrami
100 g sauerkraut, well drained

Method

Butter one side of each slice of bread. Spread the other side with Russian dressing. Layer the cheese, corned beef, and sauerkraut on two slices, dressing side up. Top with the remaining slices, butter-side out. Toast in a sandwich press or frying pan over medium heat for 5–6 minutes, until the bread is golden and crisp and the cheese has melted.

Adaptations & Substitutions

Cheese Swap: Try Gruyère, provolone, or mild cheddar.
Lighter Version: Replace half the dressing with Greek yoghurt for a tangier, lighter filling.
Extra Crunch: Add sliced pickles inside or serve them on the side.
No Russian Dressing? Mix 2 tablespoons mayonnaise, 1 tablespoon ketchup, ½ teaspoon horseradish, and a splash of Worcestershire sauce — a quick substitute that tastes spot on.

Storage

Best eaten fresh. If needed, wrap in foil and keep in the fridge for up to 1 day, then reheat in a sandwich press.

Tandoori Chicken Sandwich
with Spiced Fries

This flavour-packed sandwich is a perfect fusion of bold Indian spices and familiar deli fillings. Smoky tandoori chicken, crisp lettuce, juicy tomato, creamy tandoori mayo, and sweet mango chutney create a balance of spice, tang, and freshness. It's a proper lunch upgrade.

Makes: 6–8 servings
Prep Time: 10 minutes
Cook Time: 10 minutes
Total Time: 10 minutes

Ingredients

For the Chicken
500g cooked chicken, shredded or finely chopped
3 tablespoons tandoori paste
1 tablespoon lemon juice

For the Tandoori Mayonnaise
200g mayonnaise (whole egg mayo works best)
50g Greek yoghurt
2 tablespoons tandoori paste (adjust to taste)
½ teaspoon garlic powder
½ teaspoon paprika
½ teaspoon cumin (optional, for extra depth)
Salt and black pepper, to taste

Method

Mix the cooked chicken with the tandoori paste and lemon juice. Let it sit for 5 minutes to absorb the flavour. In a bowl, whisk together the mayonnaise, Greek yoghurt, tandoori paste, garlic powder, paprika, cumin, salt and black pepper. Stir the chicken into the tandoori mayo until well coated.

Adaptations & Substitutions

Add mixed salad leaves to rolls or flatbreads, or rocket and spinach for bagels. Add sliced cucumber for crunch.
Finish with mango chutney, either a drizzle or a spoonful.

Serving Ideas

Classic Sandwich Filler: Spread onto a soft roll, bagel, or flatbread.
Wrap It Up: Roll in a tortilla with lettuce and cucumber.
Jacket Potato Topper: Spoon over a hot, buttery baked potato.

Storage

Keeps for up to 3 days in the fridge

Spiced Fries

Makes: 2–4 servings
Prep Time: 5 minutes
Cook Time: 25 minutes (oven) or 15 minutes (air fryer)
Total Time: 30 minutes (oven) or 20 minutes (air fryer)

Ingredients

500 g potatoes, cut into thick chips (or use frozen chips as a shortcut)
2 tablespoons vegetable oil (or ghee for extra flavour)
1 teaspoon garam masala
1 teaspoon ground cumin
½ teaspoon paprika
½ teaspoon turmeric
½ teaspoon garlic powder (optional)
½ teaspoon salt (adjust to taste)
½ teaspoon chilli powder or cayenne (optional, for heat)
Fresh coriander (cilantro) chopped, as a garnish
Lemon wedges as a garnish

Method

Oven Method – Preheat oven to 220 °C. Toss potato chips in oil and spices until evenly coated. Spread on a baking tray in a single layer. Bake for 25–30 minutes, turning halfway, until golden and crisp.
Air Fryer Method – Toss potato chips in oil and spices. Air fry at 200 °C for 12–15 minutes, shaking halfway.

Pork Pies & the Perfect Pickle - Linda Davey

How to Build a Salad

Supermarket Salads: Convenient or Just a Soggy Disappointment?

We've all been there, standing in front of the supermarket fridge, eyeing up the pre-made salad section, thinking, "That looks fresh and healthy." But by the time you get it home or back to the office, what was once a promising meal has turned into a sad, wilted mess. The leaves are limp, the dressing has pooled at the bottom, and somehow, despite being full of ingredients, it still manages to taste like absolutely nothing.

Now, not all supermarket salads are a total let-down, and they are undeniably convenient. But let's be honest: **Tiny Fork, Big Effort:** Ever tried spearing a cherry tomato with one of those flimsy plastic forks? Impossible.
Mostly Lettuce: A mountain of leaves with a sad scattering of toppings.
Dressing Drama: Either too much (soggy mess) or too little (flavourless bites).
Rubbery Chicken: Why is it always so cold and chewy?

Salads have a reputation problem. They're either presented like rabbit food, a limp pile of lettuce with a lonely tomato, or they're drowning in dressing. But an excellent salad, one that's hearty, fresh, and full of flavour, can be a meal in itself.
The trick is layering it right. Follow this guide to elevate your salad game, turning it from a begrudged side dish into something you'll actually want to eat.

The Ultimate Salad Formula
Start with Greens Choose a base of lettuce, spinach, rocket, kale, or mixed leaves. A mix of crunchy and soft greens adds variety and texture.

Add Hearty Vegetables Cucumber, carrot, tomato, capsicum, radish, or beetroot, anything with crunch, colour, and bite. Boost with Beans, Pulses, Rice, or Pasta Chickpeas, kidney beans, lentils, quinoa, brown rice,and whole wheat pasta add substance and keep you full.

Include Protein A boiled egg or grilled chicken adds staying power. Or try tuna, tofu, halloumi, or falafel.

Finish with Flavour Sprinkle with cheese, nuts, seeds, or add an avocado.
Top with a homemade dressing: lemon juice, olive oil, balsamic vinegar, or a touch of honey mustard.

Quick & Easy Homemade Salad

A fresh, hearty salad that comes together in minutes and actually keeps you full.

Serves: 2
Prep Time: 10 minutes
Total Time: 10 minutes

Ingredients

2 large handfuls mixed greens(lettuce, spinach, rocket)
1 carrot, grated or julienne
6 cherry tomatoes, halved
¼ cucumber, sliced
100g cooked quinoa, brown rice, or chickpeas (use what you have)
1 boiled egg, sliced (or swap for grilled chicken, halloumi, or tofu)
¼ avocado, sliced (optional)
A sprinkle of feta, parmesan, or cheddar

For the Dressing

2 tablespoons olive oil
1 tablespoon lemon juice or balsamic vinegar
½ teaspoon mustard or honey (optional)
Salt and black pepper, to taste

Method

Chop and prepare all ingredients, then add to a large bowl.
Whisk the dressing ingredients together in a small bowl or jar.
Drizzle over the salad, toss well, and serve immediately.

Adaptations & Substitutions

Extra crunch: Add croutons or toasted seeds
Dairy-Free: Skip the cheese or swap for a vegan version.

Storage

Best served fresh, but undressed salad will keep in the fridge for 1–2 days.

Cheese & Onion Quiche

A classic British quiche with buttery, flaky pastry, sweet caramelised onions, and rich, tangy cheese. Perfect for lunch, a picnic, or a light dinner. Serve warm or at room temperature with a side salad, pickles, or chutney. When Mum asked what I wanted to eat for my 18th birthday tea, this was my request. It came to the table with mashed potatoes, tinned tomatoes, and a potato wrapped in foil with candles stuck into it. Simple, homely, and completely unforgettable! Proof that food isn't just about flavour, it's about the moments that come with it.

Makes: 1 large quiche (8 servings) **Cook Time:** 40–45 minutes **Total Time:** 1 hour 10–15 minutes
Prep Time: 30 minutes

Ingredients

For the Pastry
40g plain flour
100g butter, chilled and cubed
100g lard (swap for butter for a vegetarian version)
Cold water to mix

For the Filling
2 medium onions, finely sliced
1 teaspoon butter (for frying)
50g mature Cheddar cheese, grated
50g Red Leicester (optional, for extra colour and flavour)
3 large eggs
200ml double cream (swap for single cream or milk for a lighter version)
100ml milk
½ teaspoon salt
½ teaspoon white pepper
¼ teaspoon nutmeg (optional, enhances the flavour)

Method

Preheat oven to 180 °C. 2. In a large bowl, rub butter and lard into the flour with your fingertips until it resembles breadcrumbs. Gradually add cold water (about 4-5 teaspoons) and mix until the dough comes together. Wrap in cling film and chill in the fridge for 30 minutes.

Make the Filling
Melt butter in a pan and cook the onions over low heat for 10-15 minutes until soft and lightly golden. Let it cool. In a bowl, whisk the eggs, cream, and milk, then season with salt and pepper, and nutmeg.
Roll out the chilled pastry on a floured surface and line a 23cm tart tin. Trim the overhanging edges. Prick the base with a fork, line with baking paper and baking beans, and blind bake at 180 °C for 15 minutes. Remove the paper and baking beans, then bake for another 5 minutes until lightly golden.
Scatter grated cheese and caramelised onions over the baked pastry base. Pour over the egg and cream mixture. Bake at 180 °C for 30-35 minutes, or until golden and set in the middle.

Adaptions & Substitutions

Vegetarian? Use butter instead of lard in the pastry.
Gluten-free? Swap plain flour for gluten-free flour plus ½ teaspoon xanthan gum to help bind the dough. **Lighter version?** Use single cream or a mixture of half milk and half yogurt instead of double cream.
Different cheeses? Try Gruyère for nutty richness, Lancashire or Wensleydale for tang, or goat's cheese for extra punch. **Want to add extra flavour?** Try cooked bacon or ham for a quiche Lorraine twist, chopped leeks instead of onions, a teaspoon of English mustard in the egg mix, or a herb boost with chopped chives, thyme, or parsley.

Tips

Crisper base: Brush the pastry with a little beaten egg white after blind baking to seal it. Serving suggestion: Best served warm with a side of pickle or a fresh green salad.

Storage

Keeps in the fridge for 3 days or in the freezer for up to 1 month.

Pork Pies & the Perfect Pickle - Linda Davey

Scotch Eggs Our Bakery Classic

Mum made the best Scotch eggs, though we didn't have them often. She usually brought them out at Christmas or whenever she fancied something a bit different.
When she made them, she seasoned them properly, crisped them up beautifully, and they were full of flavour. Best of all, we ate them hot from the fryer with chips and salad cream.

Makes: 20 Scotch eggs
Prep Time: 30 minutes
Cook Time: 10-12 minutes
Total Time: Approx 40 - 50 minutes

Ingredients

1kg pork sausage meat (or good-quality pork sausages, skins removed)
2 tablespoons English mustard
1 tablespoon chopped chives
1 tablespoon chopped parsley
½ teaspoon grated nutmeg
20 medium eggs (soft-boiled for a gooey centre, or hard-boiled if preferred)
4 slices stale bread for crumbs (or use panko for extra crunch)
2 eggs, whisked (for coating)
100g plain flour (for dusting)
Vegetable or sunflower oil for deep frying

Method

Boil eggs for 5-6 minutes for a soft centre, or 9-10 minutes for fully hard-boiled. Transfer to ice-cold water, then peel carefully once cooled. In a bowl, mix sausage meat with mustard, chives, parsley, and nutmeg until well combined. Divide the mixture into 20 equal portions. Flatten one portion in your hand, place a peeled egg in the centre, and wrap the meat around it, sealing any gaps.
Roll each wrapped egg in flour, then dip into the whisked eggs, and coat in breadcrumbs.
Heat oil to 180 °C. Fry the Scotch eggs 2-3 at a time for 6-8 minutes until golden brown. Drain on kitchen paper and allow to cool slightly before serving.

Adaptations & Substitutions

More Flavour? Add thyme, sage, Worcestershire sauce, or crumble in 500g black pudding. Gluten-Free? Use gluten-free flour and breadcrumbs.

Serving Suggestions

Ploughman's Lunch: Serve with pickle, cheese, and salad. Scotch Egg Sandwich: Slice and stuff into buttered bread with mustard mayonnaise. Pub-Style Snack: Enjoy warm with a pint of ale or cider.

Storage

Keeps in the fridge for up to 3 days. Reheat in the oven to crisp them back up.

Chicken Shawarma Sandwich

Not a traditional UK flavour, but these shawarma sandwiches were an unexpected hit at The Yorkshireman's Pie and became a customer favourite. Juicy, spiced chicken, creamy garlic sauce, and crisp salad wrapped in soft flatbread made for the perfect grab-and-go lunch.

Prep Time: 5 minutes **Total Time:** 5 minutes **Makes:** 4–6 servings

Ingredients

For the Chicken Marinade
500g boneless, skinless chicken thighs (or breast)
3 tablespoons Greek yogurt
2 tablespoons olive oil
3 cloves garlic, minced
1 tablespoon lemon juice
1 teaspoon ground cumin
1 teaspoon ground coriander
1 teaspoon paprika
½ teaspoon cinnamon
½ teaspoon turmeric
½ teaspoon cayenne pepper (optional, for heat)
1 teaspoon salt
½ teaspoon black pepper

For the Garlic Sauce (Toum-Inspired)
4 tablespoons Greek yogurt or mayonnaise 2 cloves garlic, finely minced 1 tablespoon lemon juice ½ teaspoon ground cumin. Salt and pepper, to taste

For the Sandwich
Flatbreads, pita, wraps, or sandwich rolls (or use the Naan recipe from this book)
1 small red onion, thinly sliced
1 tomato, diced
½ cucumber, sliced
A handful of lettuce or shredded cabbage
Pickles (optional, but delicious)

Method

In a bowl, mix yogurt, olive oil, garlic, lemon juice, and spices. Add chicken thighs, coat well, and marinate for at least 1 hour (overnight is even better).
Heat oil in a pan over medium-high heat. Cook for 5–6 minutes per side until browned and cooked through.
Oven: Bake at 200 °C for 20–25 minutes, turning halfway.
Air Fryer: Cook at 190 °C for 12–15 minutes, flipping halfway.
Grill/BBQ: Cook over medium heat for 5–7 minutes per side until charred and cooked through.
Let the chicken rest for a few minutes, then slice thinly.
Garlic Sauce: In a small bowl, combine yogurt (or mayo), garlic, lemon juice, cumin, salt, and pepper.

Assemble

Warm your flatbread, pita, or roll in the oven at 180 °C for 3–5 minutes, until soft. Spread a layer of garlic sauce on the bread. Add lettuce, cucumber, tomato, and onion. Pile on the sliced chicken, add pickles if using, and drizzle with more garlic sauce.

Adaptions & Substitutions

Vegetarian? Use roasted cauliflower or grilled halloumi instead of chicken.
Spicier? Add extra cayenne or harissa paste to the marinade.
Gluten-free? Use gluten-free flatbreads or wrap in lettuce leaves.
Dairy-free? Swap Greek yogurt for coconut yogurt or add more olive oil.
Extra crunch? Add radishes or crispy fried onions.

Tips

Marinate chicken overnight in the fridge for the deepest flavour.
Use chicken thighs for juicier, more tender meat.
For that smoky shawarma taste, try grilling over an open flame or BBQ.

Sandwich Fillers

Cheese & Onion Sandwich Filler
Simple, tangy, and comforting, the flavour of every supermarket sandwich

Coronation Chicken Sandwich Filler
Fruity, curried, and deeply British, a Jubilee dish turned everyday favourite

Chicken, Sweetcorn & Mayonnaise Filler
Cheap, cheerful, and convenient, the one every UK supermarket stocks.

Chicken Tikka Sandwich Filler
Spiced and fragrant, a deli counter favourite with real punch.

Prawn Cocktail Sandwich Filler
A retro favourite with a hint of Christmas party nostalgia

Tuna Crunch Sandwich Filler
Creamy, crunchy, and always reliable, the quick win of fillers.

Cheese & Onion
Sandwich Filler

A classic British sandwich filling, this cheesy, tangy, and creamy mix is perfect for sandwiches, jacket potatoes, or spreading on toast. The combination of sharp Cheddar, rich Red Leicester, and fresh onions makes it bold, nostalgic, and full of flavour. It was also the most popular filler at The Yorkshireman's Pie bakery counter. No matter how many tubs we made, this was always the first to sell out. Regulars swore by it, whether tucked into a sandwich, piled high in a roll, or spooned into a jacket potato for a proper lunch.

Prep Time: 10 minutes   **Total Time:** 10 minutes   Makes: approx. 6–8 servings

Ingredients

250g Red Leicester cheese, grated
500g English Cheddar cheese, grated
1 bunch spring onions, finely chopped (including green tops)
1 brown onion, finely chopped
½ teaspoon white pepper
6 tablespoons real egg mayonnaise

Method

Finely chop brown onion and spring onions, including the green tops for colour and flavour. In a bowl, combine grated Cheddar and Red Leicester with the mayonnaise. Add white pepper and mix well until everything is evenly coated. Adjust consistency. For a thicker, chunkier mix, reduce the mayonnaise slightly.

Adaptions & Substitutions

No Red Leicester? Use Double Gloucester or extra- mature Cheddar for similar richness.
Lighter version? Swap half the mayonnaise for Greek yogurt for a tangy, lower-fat option.
Want more bite? Add a teaspoon of English mustard or a pinch of cayenne for warmth.
Egg-free? Use vegan mayonnaise for a plant-based version.
Extra freshness? Stir in chopped chives or parsley.

Serving Suggestions

Classic sandwich – spread generously between thick white or seeded bread.
Bagel Filler – pile onto a toasted bagel for an indulgent bite.
Jacket Potato Topping – spoon over a hot baked potato for a comforting lunch.
Cheesy Toast Topping – spread on crusty bread and grill for an instant cheese toastie.

Storage

Keeps for up to 5 days in the fridge

Chicken, Mayo & Sweetcorn
Sandwich Filler

If you loved that creamy chicken & sweetcorn filler from a certain UK supermarket (shhh...), this homemade version is every bit as tasty, far cheaper, and even fresher. Quick to make, comforting, and endlessly versatile, it's perfect for sandwiches, wraps, jacket potatoes, or stuffing into a lunchbox when you want something that just hits the spot.

Prep Time: 10 minutes   **Total Time:** 10 minutes   **Makes:** approx. 4–6 servings

Ingredients

2 cooked chicken breasts, finely shredded (or use pre-cooked rotisserie chicken for extra flavour)
1 small can sweetcorn (about 150g drained)
4 heaped tablespoons mayonnaise
½ teaspoon sugar (to mimic that little touch of sweetness)
Salt and white pepper, to taste

Method

In a bowl, combine the shredded chicken, sweetcorn, and mayonnaise.
Stir in the sugar, salt, and white pepper. Mix well until creamy, adding more mayonnaise if you prefer it extra saucy.
Serve straight away, or chill for 30 minutes for the best flavour.

Adaptions & Substitutions

Vegetarian alternative – Swap chicken for chickpeas, butter beans, or shredded jackfruit. Use vegan mayonnaise for a plant-based version.
Want more flavour? – Add ½ teaspoon mild curry powder for a curried version, stir in ½ teaspoon Dijon mustard, or mix through chopped spring onions or chives.
Lighter version – Replace half the mayo with low-fat yogurt or quark for a tangy, high-protein filler.
Gluten-free? – The mix itself is naturally gluten-free, just serve with gluten-free bread, wraps, or crackers (always check labels).
Creamier alternative – Mix in mashed avocado or Greek yogurt with a squeeze of lemon.

Serving Suggestions

Classic Sandwich – Layer into soft white bread or a crusty roll.
Wrap It Up – Roll into a tortilla with shredded lettuce.
Jacket Potato Topper – Spoon generously over a hot, buttery baked potato.
Deli-Style Salad – Toss with mixed leaves and cherry tomatoes for a lighter option.

Storage

Keeps for up to 3 days in the fridge.

Coronation Chicken
Sandwich Filler

Dreamt up in 1953 for Queen Elizabeth II's coronation, this dish was the brainchild of Le Cordon bleu chefs Constance Spry and Rosemary Hume. They wanted something regal yet practical: a dish they could make in advance and serve cold to hundreds of guests without losing its shine. The answer was Coronation Chicken: tender chicken in a creamy, lightly spiced sauce with just a hint of sweetness from fruit. It was British comfort with a touch of the exotic, the perfect balance of tradition and adventure on a plate. And while it might have started at a royal banquet, it quickly found its way into everyday kitchens and sandwich shops up and down the country. It is just as good in a sandwich as it is on a jacket potato, with its sweet, tangy, and gentle spices. A true lunchbox legend that still wears its crown well.

Prep Time: 10 minutes   **Total Time:** 10 minutes   **Makes:** Approx. 6 servings

Ingredients

500g shredded cooked chicken breast
250g whole egg mayonnaise
1 jar mango chutney
2 teaspoons lemon juice
1 tablespoon curry powder
1 tablespoon Dijon mustard

Method

In a bowl, mix the mayonnaise, mango chutney, lemon juice, curry powder, and Dijon mustard until smooth. Add the shredded chicken and stir until evenly coated. Cover with cling wrap and store in the refrigerator until needed.

Adaptions & Substitutions

Lighter version. Swap half the mayonnaise for Greek yogurt for a tangy, lighter option.
Spice it up. Add extra curry powder, a pinch of cayenne, or chopped fresh chilli for more heat.
Too thick? Add a splash of milk, cream, or coconut milk to loosen the texture.
Gluten-free. Naturally gluten-free (just check the chutney label).
Dairy-free. Use vegan mayonnaise.
Not a chicken fan? Try cooked turkey, prawns, or flaked salmon.
Vegetarian option. Chickpeas, roasted cauliflower, or firm tofu work beautifully.

Serving Suggestions

Sandwiches & Wraps. Tuck into soft bread, a bagel, or a tortilla.
Salad Topper. Spoon over mixed greens for a protein-packed lunch.
Jacket Potato Filling. A warm, fluffy potato topped with coronation chicken is comfort at its best.
Crusty Baguette. Pile high with lettuce and sliced cucumber for extra crunch.

Storage

Keeps for up to 5 days in the fridge.

Chicken Tikka
Sandwich Filler

If you're in the mood for something bold, creamy, and packed with flavour, you can easily make this Chicken Tikka Sandwich Filler at home. Perfect for sandwiches, wraps, or jacket potatoes, it's a game-changer that brings a spicy kick to lunch or dinner.

Prep Time: 10 minutes
Cook Time: 20 minutes
Total Time: 30 minutes
Makes: approx. 4-6 servings

Ingredients

For the Chicken Tikka
1 large chicken breast
2 tablespoons vegetable oil
1 teaspoon garam masala
1 teaspoon chilli powder
1 teaspoon cumin
I teaspoon paprika
1 teaspoon turmeric
1 teaspoon ground coriander ½ teaspoon salt

For the Filler
120g plain unsweetened yogurt (for creaminess)
120g full-fat mayonnaise (for richness)
1 red pepper(capsicum) finely diced
1 red onion, finely diced
Juice of ½ lemon
1 tablespoon fresh coriander (cilantro), finely chopped
Salt and pepper, to taste

Method

Preheat oven to 180 °C. In a bowl, combine garam masala, chilli powder, cumin, paprika, turmeric, ground coriander, and salt. Butterfly the chicken breast to create two even fillets. Coat with vegetable oil and half of the spice mix. Wrap the chicken in a foil pouch and bake for 20 minutes, or until cooked through. Allow to cool, then shred or dice.
In a large bowl, mix the yogurt, mayonnaise, lemon juice, coriander, red onion, red pepper, and the remaining spice mix.
Add the shredded chicken, stir well, and season with salt and pepper. Cover with cling film and chill until ready to serve.

Quick Method (Shortcut Version)

No time? Just mix: 1–2 tablespoons chicken tikka curry paste 250g mayonnaise 1 teaspoon lemon juice Finely chopped red onion and coriander Precooked shredded chicken

Substitutions & Adaptations

Vegetarian alternative – Swap chicken for chickpeas, tofu, or roasted cauliflower. Use vegan mayonnaise and yogurt for a plant-based version.
Want more spice? – Add ½ teaspoon cayenne pepper or a drizzle of sriracha.
Lighter version? – Use low-fat mayonnaise and yogurt.
Gluten-free? – Use gluten-free wraps, bread, or lettuce cups.
Sweeter balance? – Stir in ½ teaspoon honey or mango chutney for a milder finish.

Prawn Cocktail
Sandwich Filler

A Customer demand! Many of The Yorkshireman's Pie customers asked for this retro classic, and it quickly became another one of the most popular sandwich fillers. Whether you're spreading it onto a sandwich, stuffing a wrap, or using it as a dip, this creamy, tangy prawn mix is always a crowd-pleaser. And let's not forget it at Christmas, when it doubles as the ultimate starter, the prawn cocktail.

Prep Time: 5 minutes   **Total Time:** 5 minutes   **Makes:** approx. 4–6 servings

Ingredients

250g cooked peeled prawns (small prawns work best for sandwiches)
7 tablespoons mayonnaise
8 teaspoons ketchup
Juice of 1 lemon
3–4 teaspoons Worcestershire sauce
1 teaspoon paprika or cayenne (sweet or spicy, your choice)
Salt and black pepper, to taste

Method

In a bowl, combine the mayonnaise, ketchup, Worcestershire sauce, and lemon juice. Stir in the prawns until well coated. Season with salt, black pepper, and paprika or cayenne.
Store covered with cling film in the fridge until ready to use.

Adaptions & Substitutions

Swap prawns for chopped hearts of palm or jackfruit for a vegetarian option.
Add ½ teaspoon sriracha, Tabasco, or extra cayenne for something spicy
Stir in mashed avocado for a creamy twist.
Use half yoghurt and half mayonnaise for a lighter version.

Vegetarian Alternatives Abroad
Hearts of Palm: Found in tins in Latin American or international stores.
Jackfruit: Canned young jackfruit in brine, available in Asian supermarkets.
Chickpeas: Widely available, lightly mashed for texture.
King Oyster Mushrooms: Shredded for a meaty, seafood-like bite.
Firm Tofu: Diced or crumbled and marinated in lemon juice.

Serving Suggestions

Classic Sandwich: Soft white or brown bread with shredded lettuce.
Wrap It Up: Rolled in a tortilla with crunchy iceberg lettuce. Jacket
Potato Topper: Spoon over a hot, buttery baked potato.
Retro Prawn Cocktail: Serve in lettuce cups with lemon wedges.

Storage

Keeps for up to 3 days in the fridge

Tuna Crunch
Sandwich Filler

This simple but satisfying sandwich filler is creamy, crunchy, and packed with flavour. Whether you spread it on soft white bread, stuff it into a crusty roll, or pile it onto a baked potato, it's a quick and tasty classic. Easy as pie.

Prep Time: 5 minutes   **Total Time:** 5 minutes   **Makes:** 4–6 servings

---

Ingredients

- 1 tin tuna, drained (chunky or flaked, your choice)
- 1 small tin sweetcorn, drained (about 150g)
- ½ red onion, finely chopped
- 7 heaped tablespoons mayonnaise (adjust to taste)
- Salt and black pepper, to taste

Method

In a bowl, mix tuna, sweetcorn, red onion, and mayonnaise. Season with salt and black pepper. Adjust the mayonnaise if needed, depending on how creamy you like it.

Serve straight away or cover with cling film and chill in the fridge until ready to use.

Adaptations & Substitutions

Use mashed chickpeas or flaked jackfruit for a vegetarian option. Add ½ teaspoon Dijon mustard or a squeeze of lemon juice for more flavour.

Stir in mashed avocado in place of some mayonnaise for a creamier flavour.

Use low-fat mayonnaise or a mix of mayonnaise and Greek yoghurt for a lighter version.

Add chopped celery, cucumber, or grated carrot for extra crunch.

Serving Suggestions

Classic Tuna Crunch Sandwich: Soft bread or a crusty roll, buttered.
Wrap It Up: Rolled in a tortilla with lettuce and tomato. Jacket Potato Topper: Spoon over a hot, fluffy baked potato.
Deli-Style Salad: Toss with mixed greens and cherry tomatoes.

Storage

Keeps for up to 3 days in the fridge

Pork Pies & the Perfect Pickle - Linda Davey

Cakes & Baking

Almond Slice

Cherry Bakewell Muffins

"I was so lucky. My mum was a truly great cook! She was not only excellent at cooking meals, but she was also excellent at baking. She was a perfectionist. If things came out wrong the first time, she would try, then retry again until it was perfect. Her grandmother was a chef who was invited to cater high society weddings. Everyone wanted her. I guess my dear mother got the skills from her. How I miss her." — Filomena Martins

Baking in my kitchen is rarely serene. Flour lands in impossible places, the counters become a war zone, and at some point, I question every life choice while scraping burnt caramel off a tray. Yet despite the chaos, I keep coming back, because there's nothing quite like tasting a fresh bake straight from the oven, even if it's far from Instagram-worthy.

I realised why I keep returning to the kitchen when I remembered Mum's recipes for this book and her incredible skill with traditional meals. I thought little of it then, though her meaty gravy was impossible to resist.
Licking the plate earned a sharp telling-off from Dad, so I made do with devouring a whole loaf of bread, mopping up every drop after dinner.
Mum could conjure a perfect Sunday roast, but baking? That was another story. Her scones could have doubled as doorstops, and during the 1970s bread shortage, she attempted to make her own loaf. Everything went straight into a bowl and then the oven, so disaster was inevitable. (She probably could have built a retaining wall with it.)
But in Mum's defence, the state of her kitchen didn't help. Dad's DIY left crooked cabinets, uneven surfaces, and a split-level oven held shut with a bootlace. I kid you not.

Sweet treats were the exception rather than the rule. Treacle tart was a triumph, but most desserts boiled down to a tin of fruit cocktail with a generous pour of Nestlé Carnation Evaporated Milk.
And yet, baking isn't just about perfect cakes and pies. It's about licking the spoon when no one's looking, or when they are, but you don't care. It's about Nan's jam tarts, Mum's Sunday crumble, and the little wins that make the kitchen, chaos and all, unforgettable, not that one time you tried to make Choux pastry and ended up with something resembling a sad Yorkshire pudding rather than an éclair.

This chapter is all about no-fuss baking for busy home cooks and perfectly imperfect kitchens. The recipes use simple, reliable techniques that work every time, turning out delicious results and filling your home with the smell of something truly comforting from the oven.

Cherry Bakewell Muffins with Frangipane Filling
Muffins with a hidden almond centre, a nod to the Bakewell tart.

Belgian Buns
Sweet rolls swirled with fruit and topped with icing and a cherry.

Battenberg Cake
A chequer board sponge wrapped in a blanket of marzipan.

Chelsea Buns
Sticky, spiced fruit buns glazed to a glossy finish.

Millionaire's Shortbread (Caramel Slice)
Buttery shortbread, golden caramel, and a chocolate top.

Eccles Cakes
Flaky pastry filled with spiced currants, a true Lancashire classic.

Jamaican Ginger Cake
Dark, sticky, and spiced, the loaf that gets better with time.

Melton Hunt Cake
A dense fruit cake made for travel, keeping, and strong tea.

Our Bakery Scones
Light, fluffy scones perfect with jam and cream.

Almond Slice
A bakery tray bake layered with jam, frangipane, and flaked almonds.

Victoria Sponge
The queen of tea time, filled with jam and cream, simple yet superior.

Yorkshire Tea Loaf
Fruity, fat-free loaf steeped in proper Yorkshire tea.

Yum Yums
Twisted, glazed pastries, the doughnut's swirly British cousin.

Cherry Bakewell Muffins
with Frangipane Filling

A British classic, reimagined in muffin form. These Cherry Bakewell Muffins capture everything we ex-pats love about the famous tart: sweet cherries, almond sponge, and a drizzle of icing, but in a portable, hand-held bake that's perfect for tea breaks, lunchboxes, or sharing with friends. The hidden frangipane centre makes them extra indulgent, bringing that unmistakable Bakewell flavour to every bite.

Makes: 12 muffins
Prep Time: 20 minutes
Cook Time: 20 minutes
Total Time: 40 minutes

Ingredients

For the Frangipane
60g unsalted butter, softened
60g caster sugar
1 egg
60g ground almonds
½ teaspoon almond extract

For the Muffins
250g plain flour
100g caster sugar
2 teaspoons baking powder
60g ground almonds
150ml milk
100ml neutral oil
2 eggs
½ teaspoon almond extract
100g glacé cherries, chopped
12 teaspoons cherry jam

Topping
100g icing sugar
2 tablespoons water
12 whole glacé cherries
Flaked almonds, optional

Method

Preheat the oven to 180 °C Line a 12-hole muffin tray with paper cases.
To make the Frangipane Cream the butter and sugar in a small bowl until pale and fluffy. Beat in the egg, then fold through the ground almonds and almond extract. Set aside.
To Make the Muffin batter
Whisk together the flour, caster sugar, baking powder, and ground almonds in a large bowl.
In a jug, whisk the milk, oil, eggs, and almond extract. Fold the wet ingredients into the dry until just combined, then stir in the chopped cherries. Spoon half the batter into the paper cases. Add 1 teaspoon of jam to the centre of each, then top with a spoonful of frangipane. Cover with the remaining muffin batter.
Bake for 18–20 minutes, until golden and springy to the touch. Transfer muffins to a wire rack to cool completely.
To Decorate
Mix the icing sugar with the water to make a smooth glaze. Drizzle over the cooled muffins. Top each with a glacé cherry and a scattering of flaked almonds, if using.
Tips
For a neater look, spread the icing evenly over the tops with a spoon rather than drizzling it. Swap glacé cherries for fresh or frozen cherries when in season, but pat them dry before folding them into the batter. For an extra almond flavour, scatter some flaked almonds over the muffins before baking, rather than after. Warm the muffins slightly before eating for a "just-baked" feel, they're especially good with a cup of tea.

Storage

Store in an airtight container at room temperature for up to 3 days. Freeze (without icing) for up to 1 month.
Defrost at room temperature, then ice and decorate before serving.

Belgian Buns

Belgian buns are as close to bread-making as I'm going to get, apart from the odd focaccia. A simple enriched dough, a fruity swirl, and a rich icing on top. Straightforward, indulgent, and very bake-day friendly. Don't worry if you're new to enriched doughs; these buns are very forgiving and perfect for bakers at any level.

Makes: 8 - 10 slices
Prep Time: 45 minutes
Cook Time: 25–30 minutes
Total Time: 1 hour 30 minutes

Ingredients

For the Dough
500g strong white bread flour
75 g caster sugar
2 teaspoons salt
2 teaspoons dried active yeast
250 ml whole milk, lukewarm
1 large egg
50 g unsalted butter, softened
Water (if needed to loosen the dough)
1 teaspoon pure vanilla extract

For the Filling
100 g sultanas
2 tablespoons lemon curd
2 tablespoons apricot jam
Zest of 1 lemon
2 tablespoons finely chopped candied lemon peel (optional)

For the Icing
150g icing sugar
1–2 tablespoons water (or lemon juice for extra zest)
8–10 glacé cherries

Method

Prepare the Dough.
Combine flour, caster sugar, and salt in a large bowl. Dissolve yeast in a jug using lukewarm milk. Wait 5 minutes until frothy. With a stand mixer dough hook or by hand, mix dry ingredients, yeast mixture, egg, and vanilla.
Add softened butter. Knead for 8-10 minutes until the dough is smooth and elastic. If the dough feels tight, add water a tablespoon at a time until it is soft and tacky.
Place dough in a lightly oiled bowl. Cover with clingfilm and leave to rise in a warm spot for 1–1½ hours, or until doubled in size.

Prepare the Filling
Soak sultanas in warm water for 10–15 minutes. Drain well.
Mix drained sultanas, lemon zest, lemon curd, apricot jam, and candied peel (if using).

Shape the Buns
Punch down the risen dough. Transfer onto a lightly floured surface. Roll the dough into a rectangle, about 1 cm thick.
Spread filling evenly over dough, leaving a small border around the edges.
Roll up the dough from a long edge into a log. Pinch seam to seal. Slice the log into 8–10 equal pieces. Place cut-side up on a tray lined with parchment paper, allowing a 3cm space between them. Cover with cling wrap or a tea towel and prove buns for 30 minutes until puffy.

Bake

Preheat oven to 180 °C. Bake for 20–25 minutes until the buns are golden and cooked through. To check for doneness, tap on the bottom of the buns; they should sound hollow. Cool on a rack.
Mix icing sugar with water or lemon juice to make a thick, spoonable glaze.
For the best results, drizzle the glaze over fully cooled buns to prevent the icing from melting or becoming too runny. Then, top each bun with a glacé cherry.

Tips

Warm a teaspoon of apricot jam with a teaspoon of water and brush the mixture over the buns before icing to add extra shine.
Swap the sultanas for mixed dried fruit if desired. Alternatively, get creative with other filling options, such as chocolate chips, orange marmalade, or a sprinkling of cinnamon for a twist.
This can add a unique flavour and make these buns truly your own.

Battenberg Cake
With Homemade Marzipan

A Battenberg cake looks far more complicated than it really is. The secret is having the patience and the neat assembly rather than any tricky techniques. Wrapped in a layer of homemade marzipan, the bright checkerboard sponge makes a proper showpiece for the teatime table. This version keeps the steps simple, with a straightforward marzipan that is soft, nutty, and very satisfying to make yourself.

Makes: 1 Cake, 8-10 slices
Prep Time: 25 minutes
Cook Time: 20-25 minutes
Total Time: About 1hr 45

Ingredients

For the Cake
225g self-raising flour
1 teaspoon baking powder
200g unsalted butter, softened
200g caster sugar
4 large eggs
1 teaspoon almond extract
100g ground almonds
A few drops of pink food colouring

For the Marzipan
200g ground almonds
200g icing sugar, sifted
50g caster sugar 1 large egg white (or 2 tablespoons water for an egg-free version)
1 teaspoon almond extract

To Assemble
250g apricot jam, warmed

Method

Make the Marzipan 1. In a bowl, mix ground almonds, icing sugar, caster sugar, egg white, and almond extract. Bring together to form a dough and knead lightly on a surface dusted with icing sugar until smooth.
Wrap with cling film and set aside.

Make Cake
Heat oven to 180°C. Grease and line a 20 cm square tin.
Divide the tin into two sections using a folded piece of foil or parchment.
Cream butter and sugar together with an electric mixer until light and fluffy. Beat in the eggs one at a time, then add the almond essence.
Sift in the flour and baking powder, fold through, then stir in ground almonds.
Divide the mixture in half. Colour one half pink with a few drops of food colouring, leaving the other plain.
Spoon into each half of the tin, smooth the tops, and bake for 25-30 minutes until a skewer comes out clean.
Cool in the tin for 10 minutes, then transfer to a wire rack.

Battenberg Cake
With Homemade Marzipan

To Assemble
Trim the cakes into neat rectangles. Cut each in half lengthwise to make two pink and two yellow strips.
Warm the apricot jam in the microwave or stove top and brush onto the sides of each piece of cake. Stick them together alternating layers of pink and plain cake, then with the opposite colour in the next layer. Roll the marzipan approx 5mm thick to fit the cake and cover with apricot jam.
Place the cake on the marzipan and wrap it around the cake. Smooth gently.
Trim the ends neatly and discard the off-cuts. (Don't be silly, eat them!)

Storage
Keep the cake wrapped in baking paper and clingfilm in an airtight container for up to 3 days at room temperature, or 1 week in the fridge. Any unused homemade marzipan keeps for 2 weeks in the fridge, wrapped tightly.

Chelsea Buns

Chelsea buns are a classic British treat, and there's something comforting about biting into that sticky, sweet swirl of dough. For me, it's about the ritual. I used to pull mine apart, piece by piece, before taking a big bite. It's a bit like eating a Jaffa Cake, when you take off the orange first, then enjoy the sponge. That little ritual makes the whole thing last longer, the first taste even more satisfying. Whether you're sharing with friends or enjoying one alone with a cup of tea, Chelsea buns add a note of sweetness to any occasion.

Makes: 8-10 buns
Prep Time: 20 minutes
Proofing time: 1 hour
Cook Time: 20-25 minutes
Total Time: 1 hour 45 minutes

Ingredients

For the Dough
250g strong white bread flour
7g or 1 teaspoon instant yeast
1 teaspoon salt
30g caster sugar
25g unsalted butter, softened
1 large egg
150ml lukewarm milk
1 teaspoon water
1 teaspoon vanilla extract
Zest of 1 lemon

For the Filling
100g sultanas (or currants)
50g unsalted butter, melted
1 tablespoon caster sugar
1 teaspoon ground cinnamon
1 tablespoon honey (optional for extra stickiness)

For the Glaze
3 tablespoons caster sugar
2 tablespoons water

Method

In a large bowl, combine flour, yeast, salt, and sugar. Add butter, egg, milk, water, and vanilla. Mix to form a dough. Knead 5-10 minutes until smooth and elastic. Cover with clingfilm and let rise in a warm place until doubled, 1-1 1/2 hours.

While the dough rises, combine sultanas, melted butter, sugar, cinnamon, and honey (if using) in a bowl. Set aside. Preheat the oven to 180 °C.

Punch down risen dough. Roll out into a 25 x 30cm rectangle on a lightly floured surface. Spread filling evenly over dough. Roll dough from a long edge into a tight log. Slice into 8-10 pieces.

Place slices on a lined tray, leaving a 2-3 cm space between them. Cover with a tea towel and leave them to proof for 30-45 minutes. Bake the buns for 20-25 minutes, or until they are golden brown.

Make the Glaze

While the buns are baking, make the glaze by heating the sugar and water in a small pan over a low heat until the sugar has dissolved, and the mixture is syrupy. Brush glaze over warm buns straight from the oven.

Cool slightly before serving. Best warm and freshly glazed.

Tip

It's tempting to add more flour when the dough feels sticky. I've done it myself, but try to resist. Chelsea bun dough is inherently soft and tacky because of the milk, butter, and egg. A little extra flour is fine for shaping, but adding too much (even just 50 g) can make the buns firmer. Add too much flour, and your buns will turn out dense, not soft and pillowy.

The right balance gives you a tender texture that tears apart beautifully once baked. After the first rise, the dough becomes easier to work with. Lightly oiling your hands is very effective without interfering with the dough's texture.

Millionaire's Shortbread

Millionaire's shortbread is a classic British treat, loved for its perfect balance of buttery shortbread, sweet caramel, and smooth chocolate. In Australia, you'll more likely hear it called caramel slice, but back home the name Millionaire's shortbread always gave it a bit more glamour. The three layers, the indulgence, and the name itself all make it feel just that little bit special. It also is the bake my daughter, Ellie, made best. Her Millionaire's Shortbread was legendary at our bakery, always cut into neat squares and devoured far too quickly.
Every time I make it, I think of her steady hands and quiet focus. It proves that a good bake isn't about perfection; it's about the love you put into it.

Makes: 16–20 squares
Prep Time: 20 minutes
Cook Time: 25 minutes
Total Time: About 1 hour 15 minutes (including chilling)

Ingredients

For the Shortbread Base
250g plain flour
125 g unsalted butter, softened
75g caster sugar
Pinch of salt

For the Caramel Layer
200g unsalted butter
200g soft brown sugar
397g tin sweetened condensed milk
1 teaspoon pure vanilla extract
Pinch of sea salt, optional

For the Chocolate Topping
200g dark chocolate, or milk chocolate if preferred (cooking or regular chocolate)
50g unsalted butter

Method

Preheat the oven to 160 °C. Grease and line a 23 cm square baking tin with baking paper. Cream the butter and sugar for the shortbread until light and fluffy. Add the flour and salt, mixing until the mixture resembles coarse breadcrumbs. Tip into the prepared tin and press evenly into the base. Bake for 20–25 minutes until lightly golden at the edges. Leave to cool completely in the tin.
For the caramel, melt the butter and sugar together in a saucepan. Add the condensed milk and bring to a gentle boil, stirring constantly. Cook for 5–7 minutes, stirring, until the caramel thickens and turns golden. Stir in the vanilla and salt, if using. Pour the caramel over the cooled shortbread and spread evenly. Cool, then refrigerate for at least 2 hours until set. Melt the chocolate with the butter over a pan of simmering water, or in the microwave in short bursts. Stir until smooth, then pour over the caramel. Spread evenly. Chill for 30 minutes until the chocolate is firm. Cut into squares or rectangles with a sharp knife.

Adaptations & Substitutions

For a twist: Use white chocolate for the topping, or swirl dark and white chocolate together for a marbled effect. **Salted caramel:** Add ½ teaspoon flaky sea salt to the caramel for balance. **Gluten-free:** Swap the plain flour in the base for a gluten-free flour blend. **Nutty base:** Add 50 g finely chopped hazelnuts or almonds to the shortbread.

Tips

For neat slices, score the chocolate lightly with a knife before it sets completely, then cut through once firm. Dip your knife in hot water and wipe dry between cuts for clean edges.

Storage

Store in an airtight container at room temperature for up to 5 days. Refrigerate, but bring to room temperature before serving.

Eccles Cakes

Despite the name, they aren't really cakes at all, more like glorified fruit-filled pastries. But let's be honest, if we'd called them "Sticky Currant Puffs", they'd never have made it out of Lancashire. Flaky, buttery pastry stuffed with spiced currants, what's not to love? Eccles Cakes are a true British classic, a little hand-held piece of sticky, sugary joy. Just don't tell the people of Chorley, or we'll have a proper Lancashire pastry war on our hands. The Chorley folk have their own version, flatter, less sweet, and made with short crust pastry instead of puff, and they'll insist theirs is the original. Best not to take sides.

Makes: 8 cakes

Prep Time: 20 minutes

Cook Time: 15–20 minutes

Total Time: About 40 minutes (including cooling)

Ingredients

For the Cakes
250g frozen puff pastry, thawed
50g butter
100g currants (smaller and sweeter than raisins)
50g soft brown sugar
½ teaspoon mixed spice
½ teaspoon cinnamon
Zest of 1 lemon
1 egg white, lightly beaten

To Finish
2 tablespoons white granulated sugar

Method

Melt the butter gently in a small saucepan, then stir in the currants, brown sugar, mixed spice, cinnamon, and lemon zest. Cook for 1 minute until fragrant and the sugar has dissolved. Set aside to cool.
Cut each puff pastry sheet into 8 equal squares or circles.
Place a spoonful of the current mixture in the centre of each piece. Brush the edges with water, gather the pastry over the filling, and pinch to seal.
Turn the cakes seam-side down and flatten gently with your hand. Place on a baking tray lined with parchment paper, brush the cakes with egg white, and sprinkle with granulated sugar.
Bake at 200 °C for 15–20 minutes, until golden brown.
Allow to cool for at least 10 minutes (though everyone burns their tongue on the first one).

Adaptations & Substitutions

No currants? Use sultanas or finely chopped raisins. **Prefer a richer filling?** Add a splash of rum, brandy, or sherry. **No brown sugar?** Use white sugar with a drizzle of honey. **No lemon zest?** Try orange zest for a subtler twist.
Dairy-free? Swap butter for a dairy-free alternative. **Egg-free?** Use milk or sugar syrup instead of egg white for glazing.
Want more warmth? Add a pinch of nutmeg or ground ginger.

Tips

If the filling seeps out during baking, don't worry the caramelised edges are the best bit. Dust with icing sugar after cooling for a lightly crisp finish.
Eat while still slightly warm for the full Eccles Cake experience.

Jamaican Ginger Cake

Jamaican ginger cake is one of those classic British bakes that fills the kitchen with a warm, comforting aroma of spice. Rich, moist, and sticky with treacle and syrup, it is a cake that feels like a hug in dessert form. The secret lies in its dense texture and the way it improves as it rests, becoming chewier and stickier by the day. Whether sliced plain, spread with butter, or served with custard, this cake is pure nostalgia on a plate.

Makes: 1 loaf (900 g tin)
Prep Time: 15 minutes
Cook Time: 50–55 minutes
Total Time: About 1 hour 10 minutes (including cooling)

Ingredients

150g plain flour
1 teaspoon baking powder
1 teaspoon bicarbonate of soda
2½ teaspoons ground ginger
1 teaspoon ground cinnamon
¼ teaspoon ground cloves (optional)
50g dark muscovado sugar
50g light brown sugar
100ml vegetable oil
100g black treacle
100g golden syrup
1 large egg
150ml whole milk

Method

Preheat the oven to 160 °C. Grease and line a 900 g loaf tin with parchment paper. Gently warm the treacle, golden syrup, sugars, and oil in a saucepan until smooth. Allow to cool slightly.

In a large bowl, mix the flour, baking powder, bicarbonate of soda, and spices. Whisk the egg and milk together, then add to the dry ingredients. Stir in the cooled syrup mixture. The batter will be runny; this is normal. Pour into the prepared loaf tin and bake for 50–55 minutes, or until a skewer inserted in the centre comes out clean. Leave in the tin for 10 minutes, then turn out onto a wire rack to cool completely.

Wrap in baking paper and foil, then leave for at least 24 hours before slicing. This resting time develops the cake's signature sticky texture.

Adaptions & Substitutions

No black treacle? Use molasses for a similar depth, or increase the golden syrup for a lighter flavour.
No golden syrup? Swap with honey, though the cake will be less sticky and more fragrant.
No dark muscovado sugar? Use soft brown sugar, though you'll lose a little of the caramel richness.
Gluten-free? Substitute with a plain gluten-free-flour blend and add ½ teaspoon xanthan gum.
Dairy free? Use oat milk or almond milk in place of whole milk.

Tips

Alight glaze (icing sugar mixed with water) adds shine and extra moisture. For a more indulgent version, replace 50 ml of milk with double cream. Warm the cake slightly in the microwave before serving for a nostalgic, comforting treat.

Storage

Wrap well in clingfilm and foil, then store in an airtight tin.
Keeps for up to 5 days at room temperature, and often improves after a day or two.
Freeze for up to 1 month. Defrost at room temperature before serving.

Melton Hunt Cake

This is the sort of cake that turns up in old tin boxes on rainy day picnics and shooting lodge sideboards - dense, dark, and just sweet enough. Bakers created this no-frills fruitcake for the Melton Mowbray Hunt, making it sturdy enough to travel well and keep even better. People often wrapped it in brown paper and tucked it into saddlebags. Think of it as the cake equivalent of a countryside romp, rich with fruit, warming with spice, and always ready for strong tea.

Makes: 1 deep 20 cm round cake (or 1 large loaf)
Prep Time: 30 minutes
Cook Time: 2–2.5 hours
Total Time: About 3 hours (including cooling)

Ingredients

225g unsalted butter, softened
200g soft brown sugar (light or dark)
4 medium eggs
225g plain flour
1 teaspoon baking powder
½ teaspoon ground cinnamon
¼ teaspoon grated nutmeg
10 g glacé cherries, halved
100g chopped walnuts or blanched almonds
400 g mixed dried fruit (currants, sultanas, raisins)
Zest of 1 lemon
Zest of 1 orange
2 tablespoons milk
2 tablespoons brandy or sherry, plus extra for brushing (optional)

Method

Preheat the oven to 150 °C. Grease and line a deep 20 cm round cake tin, or use a 900 g loaf tin for a rustic finish.
Cream the butter and sugar until pale and fluffy. Beat in the eggs one at a time, adding a spoonful of flour with each to prevent curdling.
Sift in the remaining flour, baking powder, and spices, then fold in gently. Stir through the dried fruit, nuts, zests, and cherries. Add the milk and alcohol, if using, to bring the mixture together. Spoon into the prepared tin and level the top. Scatter whole almonds, if desired.
Bake for 2–2½ hours, until a skewer inserted into the centre comes out clean. Check after 1½ hours and cover loosely with foil if the cake is browning too quickly. Leave to cool in the tin. Brush with brandy while still warm for extra depth, if using.

Adaptions & Substitutions

No walnuts? Swap for pecans, hazelnuts, or leave them out entirely. **No glacé cherries?** Use dried apricots, chopped dates, or dried cranberries. **Gluten-free?** Use a plain gluten-free flour blend and add ½ teaspoon xanthan gum. **Dairy free?** Replace butter with a dairy-free spread, and milk with oat or almond milk. **Prefer a boozy cake?** Double the alcohol and feed with a drizzle every few days while stored.

Storage

Wrap in baking paper and foil, then store in a tin.
Keeps well for 1–2 weeks, and improves in flavour after a few days. Can be frozen for up to 3 months. Wrap tightly, then thaw at room temperature before serving.

Tips

For a richer flavour, soak the dried fruit overnight in tea, brandy, or sherry before baking. The cake slices neatly once rested for a day, so it's a good one to make ahead.

Clotted Cream
In Puddings & Desserts
Pg 149

Our Bakery Scones

My daughter Ellie could bake the lightest scones, the kind that stopped you in your tracks the moment they came out of the oven. Light, fluffy, and golden-topped, they were the pride of our little family bakery here in Perth, and always one of the first to disappear from the counter. We ran the bakery for a few years, and Ellie's scones quickly became a local favourite. Buttery, tender, and perfect with jam and cream, (or cream and jam, depending on which side of the debate you're on)

Makes: 8–10 scones **Cook Time:** 12–15 minutes **Total Time:** About 30 minutes
Prep Time: 15 minutes

Ingredients

350g self-raising flour, plus extra for dusting
1 teaspoon baking powder
¼ teaspoon salt
85g cold unsalted butter, cubed
3 tablespoons caster sugar
175ml whole milk
1 teaspoon vanilla extract
1 teaspoon lemon juice or white vinegar
1 egg, beaten, for glazing

Method

Preheat the oven to 220 °C. Lightly flour a baking tray or line with parchment paper.
In a large bowl, mix the flour, baking powder, sugar and salt. Rub the butter in with your fingertips until it resembles fine breadcrumbs. Warm the milk in a small pan, then stir in the vanilla and lemon juice. Let it sit for 1 minute until slightly curdled. Make a well in the dry mix, pour in the milk, and gently combine using a knife.
Turn out onto a floured surface and knead lightly until just brought together. Pat the dough to about 2.5 cm thick. Use a 5-6 cm round cutter to cut out scones, pressing straight down. Place on the baking tray, brush the tops with beaten egg, and bake for 12-15 minutes until risen and golden. Cool slightly on a wire rack and serve warm with jam and cream.

Adaptations & Substitutions

No self-raising flour? Use plain flour plus 2 teaspoons baking powder.
Dairy free? Replace milk with oat, almond, or soy milk, and glaze with a little plant milk instead of egg.
Fruit scones: Add 75 g currants, raisins, or sultanas before shaping.

Storage

Best eaten on the day of baking. Store in an airtight container at room temperature for up to 2 days. Freeze unbaked scones for up to 1 month. Bake from frozen, adding 2–3 minutes to the cook time.

Tips

Handle the dough as little as possible to keep the scones light and fluffy.
Dip the cutter in flour between cuts for clean edges. For a bakery look, place the scones close together on the tray so they rise tall.

Pork Pies & the Perfect Pickle - Linda Davey

Traditional Almond Slice
Bakery Style

A true teatime favourite, this almond slice captures the quiet joy of home baking. A buttery short crust base, a generous layer of jam, and a soft, fragrant frangipane topping come together in perfect harmony, finished with flaked almonds and a golden bake. It's the kind of tray bake that feels both nostalgic and a little bit fancy, equally at home on a cake stand or tucked into a lunchbox. One bite and you'll see why this classic never goes out of style.

Makes: 12 slices **Cook Time:** 30-35 minutes **Total Time:** About 55 minutes
Prep Time: 20 minutes

Ingredients

For the Base
200g plain flour
100g cold unsalted butter, cubed
2 tablespoons caster sugar
1 egg yolk
1-2 tablespoons cold water

For the Filling
100g unsalted butter, softened
100g caster sugar
2 eggs
100g ground almonds
1 tablespoon plain flour
½ teaspoon almond extract, optional
3 tablespoons raspberry jam, or cherry jam
Flaked almonds, for topping
Icing sugar, for dusting, optional

Method

Preheat the oven to 180 °C. Grease and line a 20 cm square tin with baking parchment, leaving some overhang to help lift the slice out after baking.
Rub the butter into the flour until it resembles breadcrumbs.
Stir in the sugar, then add the egg yolk and just enough water to form a soft dough.
Press into the tin and prick with a fork. Chill in the fridge for 10 minutes.
Bake the base for 10 minutes to help keep it crisp. Allow to cool and then spread the jam evenly over the pastry.
Sift the flour and set aside. Beat butter and sugar until pale and fluffy. Add the eggs one at a time, whisking well after each addition. Fold through the flour until just combined.
Stir in the ground almonds and almond extract. Spread the frangipane mixture over the jam and level the top. Scatter with flaked almonds.
Bake for 30-35 minutes until golden and just set. A skewer should come out clean from the centre. Cool in the tin, then lift out and slice into 12 bars. Dust with icing sugar if using.

Adaptations & Substitutions
Pastry shortcut: Use ready-rolled shortcrust pastry to save time.
Jam swaps: Apricot, cherry, or blackcurrant jam all work beautifully.
No flaked almonds? Sprinkle with demerara sugar before baking for crunch.

Storage
Store in an airtight container at room temperature for up to 4 days.
Freeze: Wrap well with cling film and freeze for up to 1 month. Defrost unwrapped at room temperature before serving.

Tips
For neat slices, cool completely before cutting. For a softer base, skip blind baking, for a crisper finish, don't. Serve slightly warm with custard for a pudding-style treat.

Victoria Sponge

If there's one cake that know sit's the queen of the tea table, it's the Victoria sponge. Light, fluffy, and dressed up with jam and cream, it's simple yet smugly superior, the sort of bake that doesn't need frosting or frills to steal the show. Perfect for settling the age-old debate of which comes first: the jam or the cream? It's just the thing to make you feel a little posh, even if you're eating it in your slippers.

Makes: 8-10 slices
Prep Time: 15 minutes

Cook Time: 20-25 minutes (two tins) or 30-40 minutes (one deep tin)

Total Time: About 1 hour 15 minutes (including cooling)

Ingredients

For the Sponge
200g butter or margarine, softened
200g caster sugar
200g self-raising flour
4 large eggs
½ teaspoon pure vanilla essence

For the Buttercream
150g butter or margarine, or dairy-free alternative
300g icing sugar
1 teaspoon vanilla essence

To Finish
Jam, strawberry or raspberry
Icing sugar, for dusting

Method

Grease two 18cm round cake tins and line the bases with baking paper. If using one deep tin, line the sides as well.
Cream the butter with a whisk or stand mixer until soft, then beat in the sugar until pale and fluffy. This traps air, helping the sponge rise. Sieve the flour. Add the eggs one at a time, whisking well after each addition. Fold in the flour and vanilla gently, mixing until combined. Divide the mixture evenly between the tins and smooth the tops.
Bake at 190 °C for 20-25 minutes (two tins) or 30-40 minutes (one deep tin). Test with a skewer; if it comes out clean, the sponge is ready. Cool in the tins for 5 minutes, then turn out onto a wire rack. If using one deep tin, slice in half when cooled.

Make the Buttercream and Assemble
Beat the butter, icing sugar, and vanilla together with a whisk until light and fluffy.
Spread jam over one sponge, then top with buttercream. Place the second sponge on top. Dust with icing sugar before serving.

Adaptions & Substitutions

Dairy-free? Use dairy-free margarine and fill with coconut cream instead of buttercream. **Gluten-free?** Use a gluten-free self-raising flour blend and add ½ teaspoon xanthan gum.

Tips

Use real butter for extra richness. Swap buttercream for whipped double cream for a classic filling. Always cool the sponges fully before filling, or the buttercream will melt.
Add sliced strawberries or raspberries to the jam for extra indulgence.

Storage

Store in an airtight container at room temperature for up to 2 days. Best eaten fresh, but can be frozen unfilled for up to 1 month. Defrost, then add filling before serving.

Yorkshire Tea Loaf

This Yorkshire Tea Loaf was a firm favourite at our bakery, The Yorkshireman's Pie, rich with tea-soaked fruit brewed with proper Yorkshire tea. Customers often bought all of it, especially when they found out how good it tasted toasted and slathered in butter. Humble yet quietly show-stealing, it's simple, comforting, and full of old-fashioned flavour. Technically, there's no butter or fat in the loaf itself, so you could almost call it fat free... though that claim disappears the moment you add the knob of butter it deserves. You should keep the kettle warm and the butter close, whether you are baking this loaf for the first time or revisiting it.

Makes: 8–10 slices
Prep Time: 10 mins (plus soaking time)

Cook Time: 1 hour

Total Time: 1 hr 10 mins
(+ overnight soak recommended)

Ingredients

300g mixed dried fruit (e.g. raisins, sultanas, currants)
250ml hot strong Yorkshire tea (2 tea bags brewed in hot water)
100g dark brown sugar
1 large egg, beaten
225g self-raising flour
½ teaspoon mixed spice (optional)
Pinch of salt

Method

Place the dried fruit in a mixing bowl and pour over the hot tea. Stir in the sugar while warm. Cover with a tea towel and leave to soak, ideally overnight, or at least 4 hours.
Preheat your oven to 180 °C. Grease and line with parchment paper a 2lb loaf tin. 9 × 5 × 3 inches.
Add the egg to the soaked fruit and tea mixture, then stir in the flour, salt, and mixed spice, if using. Mix until just combined; don't overwork.
Pour the mixture into your prepared tin and level the top.
Bake for 1 hour, or until a skewer comes out clean. If the top browns too quickly, cover with foil halfway through.
Let cool in the tin for 10 minutes before turning onto a wire rack.
Best served sliced, buttered, and alongside a proper cuppa.

Adaptions & Substitutions

You can use any mix of dried fruit you have on hand. Chopped dates or apricots give a softer bite. A little grated orange zest adds a brighter note. If you like a firmer loaf, reduce the tea by a small splash. For extra warmth, add a little more mixed spice, though the loaf is good without it.

Storage

Let the loaf cool fully, then wrap in baking paper and keep in an airtight tin for up to five days. The flavour deepens after the first day. It also freezes well. Wrap tightly and freeze for up to three months. Defrost at room temperature and slice once thawed.

Yum Yums

Not everyone outside Britain will know what a Yum Yum is, but once you've had one, you'll never forget it. Imagine a soft, twisted doughnut, golden fried, sticky with glaze, and with just the right balance of fluffy inside and crispness outside. That's a Yum Yum. A proper British indulgence, found in bakeries up and down the high street, usually in a paper bag that never makes it home intact. When we first started selling them at our bakery, even customers who'd never heard of a Yum Yum became instant converts, abandoning the traditional ring doughnuts in favour of these twisted, sticky delights. They're light, sweet, and dangerously moreish - the sort of treat that disappears before the kettle's boiled.

Prep Time: 25 minutes (plus proving)
Cook Time: 10 minutes
Total Time: About 2 hours 30 minutes (including proving)
Makes: 8 Yum Yums

Ingredients

For the Dough
500g strong white bread flour
7g dried yeast
10g salt
50g caster sugar
250 ml warm milk
50g unsalted butter, melted
1 egg
Vegetable or sunflower oil for deep frying

For the Glaze
250g icing sugar
3-4 tablespoons water
1 teaspoon vanilla extract (optional)

Method

Make the Dough
In a large bowl, combine the flour, yeast, sugar, and salt, keeping the salt and yeast on separate sides of the bowl at first. Add the warm milk, melted butter, and egg. Mix to form a soft dough.
Knead for 8-10 minutes until smooth and elastic. Cover with clingfilm and leave to rise for 1 hour, or until doubled in size.
Roll the dough into a rectangle about 1cm thick. Cut into 8 equal strips, twisting each one, and pinch the ends to hold the twist shape. Place on a baking tray lined with parchment paper. Cover with a tea towel and leave to prove for 30-45 minutes until puffed.
Heat the oil in a deep pan to 170 °C. Fry 2-3 at a time for 2-3 minutes per side, turning them with a slotted spoon until golden. Drain on a wire rack with kitchen paper underneath.

Glaze
Mix the icing sugar with enough water to make as smooth, pourable glaze. Add vanilla if using. Brush or dip the Yum Yums while still warm. Leave for a few minutes to set before serving.

Adaptations & Substitutions

Spiced dough: Add 1 teaspoon ground cinnamon or mixed spice to the dough for a festive twist. **Mini Yum Yums:** Cut the dough into 16 strips instead of 8 for smaller, bite-sized treats.

Tips

Using a cooking thermometer, keep the oil steady at 170-180 °C to avoid greasy results. Twist the dough carefully for a soft, pillowy centre. Best eaten fresh, but will keep in an airtight container for up to 2 days.

Storage

Store in an airtight container at room temperature for up to 2 days. Not suitable for freezing once glazed.

Pork Pies & the Perfect Pickle - Linda Davey

Puddings & Desserts

> "I think my mum must have been a saint; she had a husband and five daughters to feed. We had a hot, cooked dinner every single day, plus a different pudding each day. There weren't many cakes, but we enjoyed Bread Pudding, Bakewell Tart, and Lemon Meringue Pie. Spotted Dick, Syrup Sponge, Apple Pie, and Rhubarb Sponge were always served with custard. We always went home for lunch, and the daily question was never 'What's for dinner?' but 'What's for pudding, Mum?'" — Janet Mills

Looking back on my school days in the late 1960s, I can't help but chuckle at the canteen cooks as they insisted on using up every last bit of suet. Jam Roly-Poly and Spotted Dick were frequently served.

My absolute favourite was Chocolate Crunch (or as some of us affectionately called it, Concrete). It was often so overcooked that biting into it would result in a room full of jarring drills and a dentist who didn't seem to care about my suffering! Compared to the canteen cooks' barely passable pastry skills, Mum's short crust was in a league of its own.

I truly believe anyone can whip up a great pastry using her simple method that involves cold water and a half-and-half fat ratio. One of my all-time favourite desserts was her Treacle Tart.
Long before Harry Potter made it famous in *Harry Potter and the Half-Blood Prince* Chapter 9, Mum had been serving us this delightful tart for tea for years. That lovely crust paired with a sweet, chewy centre was simply unforgettable! She had a few fantastic recipes tucked away in her apron pocket, and Treacle Tart was definitely among them.

We rarely have pudding after a meal, unless it's a special occasion, but when I make one linked to old memories, it always brings with it a wave of nostalgia.
Pudding is a lovely treat now and then! As I'm writing this, I'm warming up some leftover rhubarb crumble, and I couldn't be happier!

Clotted Cream or Not Clotted Cream
A quick, creamy alternative for when real clotted cream is impossible to find in your local supermarket.

Blackberry & Apple Cobbler
Tart apples and juicy blackberries baked beneath a golden cobbler topping, best demolished with custard or cream.

Bread & Butter Pudding
Layers of buttery bread, dried fruit, and marmalade baked in rich custard until golden and comforting.

Classic British Trifle
Layers of sponge, jelly, fruit, custard, and cream—joy in a bowl and a party table classic.

Chocolate Crunch with Pink Custard
A nostalgic school dinner favourite crisp chocolate slab paired with that unforgettable pink custard.

Mum's Treacle Tart
Sticky golden syrup and bread crumbs in crisp pastry, with lemon zest and a lot of memories.

Queen of Puddings with Almond & Lavender Syrup
The school dinner classic reimagined with an almond base, jam, meringue, and a floral drizzle.

Raspberry Fool with Mascarpone
The easiest pudding ever with whipped cream and tart raspberries swirled into soft, fruity clouds.

Custard Tarts (Traditional)
Light pastry filled with silky custard, sprinkled with nutmeg

DIY Viennetta
A retro freezer favourite recreated at home with layers of vanilla ice cream and crisp chocolate.

Clotted Cream or Not Clotted Cream?

That Is the Question

Finding clotted cream outside of the UK can be a challenge. Many countries require pasteurisation by law, so producers there cannot use unpasteurised milk to make traditional clotted cream. Pasteurisation changes the flavour and texture of the milk, which is why most substitutes can't quite match the thick, luxurious richness of traditional farmhouse clotted cream. You can sometimes find imported tubs, but they're usually expensive and scarce. If you're craving a substitute (because who has time to make clotted cream from scratch?), you can make a shortcut version that captures the essence of the real thing, thick, creamy, and wonderfully indulgent.

Prep Time: 10 minutes **Total Time:** 40 minutes **Makes:** About 300ml

Chill Time: 30 minutes (recommended)

Ingredients

240ml heavy cream
(or double cream if available)
2 tablespoons mascarpone
(for thickness and creaminess)
1 tablespoon icing sugar
(optional for sweetness)
1 teaspoon pure vanilla extract
(optional for extra flavour)

Method

Place cream and mascarpone in a mixing bowl. Beat with a whisk or hand mixer until thickened but still spreadable, about 3–5 minutes. If you prefer slightly sweeter, add icing sugar and vanilla, then whisk again until smooth. Chill in the fridge for 30 minutes before serving allowing it to firm slightly.

Adaptations & Substitutions

Cheese Alternative: As a cheese alternative, mascarpone gives the smoothest texture, but use cream cheese if you have it on hand.

No icing sugar? Blitz granulated sugar briefly to avoid graininess. Chilling helps give the mixture a more "clotted" texture, making it easier to spoon onto scones.

Tips

Any cream with at least 36% fat works well. In Australia and New Zealand, use pure cream or thickened cream. In the US, heavy cream or whipping cream is the best option.

Try coconut cream whipped with a spoonful of vegan cream cheese for richness.

Add a touch of orange zest, almond extract, or even a drizzle of honey for something different.

Storage

Keep covered in the fridge for up to 3 days. Stir gently before serving if it firms up too much. Not suitable for freezing.

Blackberry & Apple Cobbler

My friends and I would go blackberry picking during the late '70s in July. Brambles stuck to our socks, our fingers turned purple, and our arms bore the scratches of a successful harvest.

We always reached for the biggest berries, convinced they would be the sweetest (even when they weren't). Half the joy was in the hunt, the rest in the sneaky eating along the way. Somehow the overflowing tubs were never quite as full by the time we arrived home. Another full harvest arrived at Nan's house. The heavily laden boughs of her neighbour's apple tree hung over the fence. No one ever said anything, but those windfalls had a funny way of ending up in her kitchen.

She'd stew them with sugar and a sprinkling of cinnamon, and more often than not, she'd make a cobbler. Simple, warm, and ladled into pudding dishes accompanied by a jug of custard on the table. It wasn't a fancy dessert, but it didn't need to be, the tart fruit bubbling beneath the soft golden, topping. Cobbler is the sort of pudding that forgives heavy-handed measuring and welcomes second helpings. It relies upon a memory, a bit of make-do, and all the warm, syrupy joy of late summer afternoons.

Prep Time: 10 minutes
Cook Time: 35-40 minutes
Total Time: Approx 50 minutes
Makes: 6 (or 4 if you're feeling emotionally fragile)

Ingredients

For the Fruit Filling
300g blackberries
2 large cooking apples (Granny Smith is an excellent substitute for a Bramley).
75g caster sugar
1 tablespoon plain flour
Juice of ½ lemon
Pinch of ground cinnamon (optional)

For the Cobbler Topping
175g self-raising flour
75g cold butter, cubed
50g caster sugar
1 egg
2-3 tablespoons milk
Demerara sugar, for sprinkling

Method

Preheat oven to 180 °C. Lightly butter a medium oven dish. Peel and chop the apples. In a bowl, toss blackberries, sugar, flour, lemon juice, and cinnamon. Spread fruit evenly in the dish.

Rub butter into the flour until it resembles breadcrumbs. Stir in the caster sugar. Whisk egg with 2 tablespoons of milk. Mix into the dry ingredients to make a soft dough, adding extra milk if needed.

Spoon or shape dollops of dough over the fruit. No need for precision here.

Brush with milk and sprinkle with Demerara sugar. Bake for 30-35 minutes, until golden and bubbling at the edges.

Serve warm with custard, cream, or vanilla ice cream.

Adaptations & Substitutions

Granulated sugar works fine; blitz it briefly for a finer texture. Salted butter is fine; just leave out extra salt. Swap in tinned peaches, fresh berries, or stewed apples. Frozen fruit can go straight in, just toss with sugar and 1 teaspoon cornflour. Any milk works; whole milk gives the richest flavour, but oat or almond milk are good alternatives.

Tips

Spoon the dough on loosely rather than smoothing it out — it bakes up lighter that way. Serve straight from the oven for the best results.
For a crunchier top: Add an extra sprinkle of Demerara sugar before baking.

Storage

Store covered in the fridge for up to 3 days. Reheat in the oven at 160 °C for 10-15 minutes before serving. Not suitable for freezing once baked, as the fruit and topping can turn soggy.

Bread & Butter Pudding
A pudding I almost didn't make

As a child, anything with "bread and butter" in the name sounded dreadful to me. But when we made it at the bakery, drenched in proper custard, it turned out to be rich, comforting, and absolutely delicious. What started off sounding like a frumpy old-school pudding became golden-topped, creamy-centred, and downright lovely. Humble, yes, but Bread and Butter pudding is rich and nostalgic, the kind of pudding that makes you feel right at home (or back at school), but in the best possible way.

Prep Time: 20 minutes
Cook Time: Approx 1 hour
Total Time: Approx 50 minutes
Makes: : 6–8

Ingredients

2–3 medium loaves thick-sliced white bread
225g butter
225g caster sugar
600ml double cream (not single or whipping cream)
570ml full cream milk
500g mixed dried fruit- soaked overnight in just enough water to cover 8 medium eggs
6 drops pure vanilla essence
454g jar marmalade

Method

Melt the butter gently in a pan and set aside. Warm the marmalade on the stove until runny.
Trim crusts from the bread and cut each slice in half. Lightly brush a large oven-proof dish with butter. Arrange a layer of bread in the base and sides of the dish, pressing down gently.
Brush with butter, scatter with some soaked fruit, sprinkle with sugar, and drizzle with marmalade.
Continue layering bread, fruit, butter, and marmalade to use up all the ingredients. Finish with fruit, butter, and marmalade on top, pressing down lightly.
In a large bowl, whisk eggs, remaining sugar, vanilla, cream, and milk until smooth. Pour over the pudding until the bread is well soaked. Leave to stand for 5 minutes.
Preheat oven to 180 °C. Place the dish in a shallow roasting tin and add 1cm of hot water to the tin to create a steam bath. Bake for 35–40 minutes, covering with baking parchment halfway if the fruit is browning. Serve warm with custard.

Adaptations & Substitutions

Extra Richness: Use brioche or hot cross buns. **Dairy-Free:** Use plant-based milk and cream, and dairy-free spread instead of butter.
Gluten-Free: Use gluten-free bread.

Tips

Best Texture: Let the custard soak into the bread properly before baking.
For an Easter Twist: Hot cross buns make this pudding spectacular. Place the baking dish in a water bath.

Storage

Store covered in the fridge for up to 3 days. Reheat in the oven at 160 °C for 15 minutes, or until warmed through. Not suitable for freezing once baked, as the custard can split.

Classic British Trifle

This recipe brings my nan's trifle back to life, layer by glorious layer. It's the sherry-soaked sponge at the bottom that does it for me, soft and just boozy enough to feel a little cheeky. Then came the fruit, the wobbly jelly that always stuck to the spoon, and the silky custard she poured with absolute precision. A cloud of whipped cream crowned the lot, finished with hundreds and thousands scattered like confetti. If you want to elevate your trifle, lean into the decadence. Use proper sponge fingers that soak up every drop, a generous splash of Harvey's Bristol Cream, thick custard, and softly whipped cream. The result isn't just a dessert, it's the kind of pudding people hover around, spoons at the ready, waiting for their turn to dive in.

Prep Time: 30 minutes to 1 hour
Chill Time: 2-4 hours or overnight
Total Time: Approx 3-5 hours (including chilling)
Serves: 6-8

Ingredients

For the Sponge
1 small Madeira cake or Swiss roll, sliced
3 tablespoons sherry, optional (or orange juice for a non-alcoholic version)

For the Fruit & Jelly Layer
1 packet raspberry or strawberry jelly
300g mixed berries (raspberries, strawberries, blackberries)

For the Custard
4 egg yolks
50g caster sugar
2 tablespoons cornflour
500ml whole milk
1 teaspoon pure vanilla extract

For the Topping
300ml double cream
1 tablespoon icing sugar
1 tablespoon sherry (optional)
25g flaked almonds, toasted
Grated dark chocolate or crushed Amaretti biscuits, to serve

Method

Layer the sponge on the bottom of a glass trifle bowl. Drizzle with sherry or orange juice and set aside. Prepare jelly according to packet instructions. Scatter the berries over the sponge and pour the jelly on top. Chill until fully set. In a medium saucepan, whisk the egg yolks, sugar, and cornflour until smooth. In a separate pan, gently heat the milk and vanilla until just steaming.

Slowly pour the hot milk into the yolk mixture, whisking constantly to prevent curdling. Return the mixture to the saucepan and cook over low heat, stirring, until it thickens and coats the back of a spoon.

Set the custard aside for a few minutes to cool slightly, it should still be pourable but not hot. Pour the warm custard gently over the fully set jelly layer. Chill again until the custard is firm and lightly wobbly.

Adaptations & Substitutions

Swap homemade custard for Bird's custard to keep it quick and nostalgic. Replace sherry with orange juice, apple juice, or even cranberry juice for a festive twist. Retro Version: Use tinned fruit cocktail or layer in poached pears, peaches, or mango for something lighter.

Leave out the almonds and decorate with sprinkles, extra berries, or crushed meringue. Gluten-Free: Use gluten-free sponge cake or Swiss roll. **Dairy-Free:** Use plant-based cream, custard, and sponge for a fully dairy-free version. **Jaffa Style:** Try orange jelly with chocolate shavings, or use cherry-flavoured jelly with Kirsch brandy for a Black Forest feel.

Tips

Always let the jelly set completely before adding the custard, or the layers will blur. Pipe the cream for a neater finish, or just spoon it on for a rustic look. For extra richness, fold a spoonful of mascarpone into the whipped cream.

Storage

Store covered in the fridge for up to 2 days. Not suitable for freezing, as the jelly and custard will separate.

Chocolate Crunch
(Chocolate Concrete) with Pink Custard

Chocolate Crunch was a proper school-dinner classic, the pudding that turned up in chipped bowls with a generous splash of pink custard. The canteen always smelled faintly of boiled cabbage and cheap cocoa, a scent you could pick up from halfway down the corridor. When they made it properly, it was glorious. Cocoa-rich, melting like shortbread, and best drowned in a pool of pink custard. That soft, pink custard we all remember so fondly wasn't custard at all, but unset strawberry blancmange (oops). Still, it had its charm. Here's how to bring back that magic without risking a broken tooth.

Prep Time: 15 minutes **Bake Time:** 18–20 minutes **Serves:** 12 squares
Chill Time: 30 minutes **Custard Time:** 10 minutes **Total Time:** Approx 45 minutes

---

Ingredients

For the Chocolate Crunch
200g plain flour
200g caster sugar
50g butter and 50g lard
(or use 100 g butter for a softer texture)
50g cocoa powder
Pinch of salt

For the Pink Custard
5 tablespoons cornflour
3 tablespoons sugar
A few drops pink food colouring
½ teaspoon strawberry extract or essence
500 ml milk

Method

Preheat oven to 180 °C. Grease and line a brownie tin 20 × 20 cm (8 × 8 in) with baking parchment. In a large bowl, combine flour, sugar, cocoa, and salt. Melt butter and lard gently, then stir into dry ingredients. Rub together with your fingertips until the texture resembles coarse crumbs. Press mixture evenly into the prepared tin. Bake for 18–20 minutes, until the edges are firm but the centre still has a little softness. Sprinkle with a little caster sugar while warm. Score into squares, then leave to cool completely in the tin before cutting to serve In a bowl, mix cornflour, sugar, colouring, and strawberry extract. Blend with a splash of milk until smooth. Heat remaining milk in a saucepan until steaming, then whisk gradually into the paste. Return to the pan and stir over medium heat until it thickens to a custard consistency, about 2–3 minutes. Pour the custard generously over the Chocolate Crunch and enjoy warm.

Adaptations & Substitutions

All Butter: Using all butter gives a softer, richer flavour, while lard makes it crisper. **Flavour Swap:** Swap strawberry essence for raspberry, or use vanilla for a milder custard.

Tips

Don't over bake the concrete; it should be crisp but not rock hard. Score the portions while warm to make it easier to cut in to neat slices. For a stronger pink colour, add the colouring drop by drop until the desired shade is reached.

Storage

Store the Chocolate Crunch in an airtight tin for up to 5 days.
The custard is best made fresh, though it will keep in the fridge for 2 days. Reheat gently, whisking to restore smoothness. Not suitable for freezing.

Mum's Treacle Tart

Mum's treacle tart was the stuff of legends, mainly because no one could quite figure out how she stretched a tin of golden syrup across so many bakes. The tart had the perfect balance of sticky sweetness and crisp pastry, with just enough lemon to stop your teeth from curling. Served warm with custard (or if you were lucky, a scoop of ice cream), it was pure comfort on a plate. Of course, as kids, we didn't care who made it or how, we just knew when you got a slice from the edge, you'd be wrestling with the stickiest bit for the next ten minutes.
And honestly, that was half the fun.

Prep Time: 15 minutes
Cook Time: 50 minutes

Total Time: 1 hour 20 minutes

Serves: 8 people if cut into neat wedges.

Ingredients

For the Pastry
300g plain flour
75g unsalted butter
75g lard
1 teaspoon salt
100ml cold water

For the Filling
750g golden syrup
250g day-old breadcrumbs
Grated zest and juice of 1 lemon

Method

Preheat oven to 190 °C. Place flour and salt in a bowl and mix evenly. Add butter and lard, then rub together until the texture resembles coarse breadcrumbs. Gradually add cold water, a small amount at a time, until a pliable dough takes shape. Shape into a ball, cover with cling film, and refrigerate for a minimum of 30 minutes.
On a lightly floured surface, roll out the pastry to suit a 23 cm (9 inch) tart tin with a removable base, allowing a slight overhang. Press into the tin, pierce with a fork, and chill for an additional 10 minutes.
Cover the pastry with baking paper and fill with baking beans.
Bake at 190 °C for 10 to 15 minutes. Carefully remove the baking beans and paper, then bake for another 5 minutes.
Gently heat the golden syrup with the lemon zest and juice in a saucepan until it becomes fluid. Mix in the breadcrumbs thoroughly, then take off the heat. Pour the warm mixture into the tart case and smooth it out evenly. Bake at 190 °C for 20 to 25 minutes, until the pastry turns golden, and the filling turns a light brown colour.
Allow to cool slightly before serving.

Adaptations & Substitutions

Golden Syrup: If you can't find the Tate & Lyle brand, supermarket's own brand works just as well.

Tips

For something fancy, cut strips of pastry, twist them, and lay them over the tart, sealing the ends with water before baking. It looks impressive with little effort.Serve with custard, cream, or vanilla ice cream for the perfect finish.

Storage

Store covered with foil at room temperature for 2 days or in the fridge for up to 4 days. Best served warm. Can be frozen for up to 2 months; thaw and reheat in the oven before serving

Queen of Puddings
with Almond & Lavender Syrup

If you went to school in the 1960's -1970's UK, chances are you've encountered Queen of Puddings at least once, whether you loved it or, like me, tried to scrape it off your plate when the dinner lady wasn't looking. This recipe is for a proper British pudding: a custard breadcrumb sponge covered with a layer of jam (raspberry if you were lucky), and topped with fluffy. Sweet, comforting, and a little over the top, it was fuel for playground mischief. The meringue sometimes arrived weepy and sad, but when it cooked properly, it was a warm, jammy hug that tasted like school days and clattering trays. This version uses almonds for a rich, nutty base, balanced with a floral lavender syrup. Almond and lavender might sound like an unusual duo, but they pair beautifully - the floral note lifts the richness of the almond without overpowering it. A little more refined than the dinner hall version, but it still has that unmistakable school-days magic.

Prep Time: 20 minutes   **Chill Time:** 10 minutes   **Makes:** 6-8 portions.

Cook Time: 45-50 minutes   **Total Time:** 1 hour 20 minutes

Ingredients

For the Almond Base
150g ground almonds
100g caster sugar
3 large eggs, separated
200 ml full-cream milk
1 teaspoon pure vanilla extract
1 tablespoon melted butter
Pinch of salt

For the Jam Layer
200 g raspberry or strawberry jam

For the Meringue Topping
3 egg whites
150g caster sugar
1 teaspoon cornflour
1 teaspoon vanilla extract

For the Lavender Syrup
1 tablespoon dried lavender flowers (culinary grade)
100 g caster sugar
100 ml water

Method

Preheat oven to 160 °C. Grease a 20cm baking dish and line with baking paper. Whisk ground almonds, sugar, and egg yolks in a bowl. Stir in milk, vanilla, melted butter, and salt until smooth. Pour into the dish and bake for 25-30 minutes, until set and golden.

While the base bakes, whisk egg whites to soft peaks. Gradually add the sugar, a spoonful at a time, until glossy. Fold in cornflour and vanilla.

Once the almond base has cooled slightly, spread with jam.

Spoon meringue over the top and spread evenly. Return to the oven for 15-20 minutes, until the meringue is golden.

Make the Lavender Syrup.

Heat the sugar and water in a small pan until dissolved. Add the lavender and simmer for 3-5 minutes.
Strain and cool completely.
Drizzle the lavender syrup lightly over the pudding or serve on the side.

Adaptions & Substitutions

Flavour: Raspberry is traditional, but cherry or blackcurrant adds depth. Old School Version: Replace ground almonds with fine fresh breadcrumbs for the old-school version.

No Lavender Syrup? You can use rosewater instead of lavender syrup.

Tips
Add the sugar to the meringue slowly for maximum gloss and stability.
Use homemade jam for the richest flavour.
For a stronger lavender flavour, leave the flowers to infuse in the syrup for 10 minutes before straining.

Storage
Best eaten on the day it's made. Store leftovers in the fridge for up to 2 days. Not suitable for freezing

Raspberry Fool with Mascarpone
The Easiest Dessert you'll Ever Make

This dessert sounds fancy, but with a name like 'fool', it's anything but complicated. Raspberry Fool is one of the simplest, dreamiest British puddings: softly whipped cream swirled with tart raspberries and just enough sugar. No baking, no faffing, just a light, fruity dessert that feels far fancier than the effort required.
Your nan might have made this kind of dish quickly when she needed a pudding, especially if she had a tin of raspberries hidden away in the cupboard. Fresh raspberries make it extra special, but the beauty of a fool is its utter fuss-free nature. Spoon it into fancy glasses for a dinner party or dollop it into bowls for a midweek treat; either way, it's simple, sweet, and delicious.

Prep Time: 15 minutes
Chill Time: 15 minutes
Total Time: Approx 30 minutes
Makes: 4 desserts

Ingredients

250g raspberries (fresh or frozen, thawed)
50g caster sugar (adjust to taste)
1 tablespoon lemon juice (optional)
125g mascarpone
150 ml double cream
½ teaspoon vanilla extract
1 tablespoon icing sugar

Method

Mash or blend the raspberries with caster sugar and lemon juice. For a smooth texture, pass through a sieve to remove seeds. Whip the mascarpone and cream together. In a bowl, whisk the mascarpone, double cream, icing sugar, and vanilla until soft peaks form. Gently fold in the raspberry purée. Fold lightly for a marbled effect or mix fully for a uniform colour. Spoon into glasses and chill for at least 30 minutes before serving.

Adaptions & Substitutions

Fruit: Try blackberries, gooseberries, or rhubarb compote for a seasonal twist. **Dairy-Free:** Use coconut cream whipped with a dairy-free cream cheese alternative. **Lighter Options:** Swap mascarpone for Greek yoghurt for a tangier, lighter dessert.

Tips

Make the fool up to 24 hours in advance and chill it until needed. Taste the raspberry purée before folding in to the cream mixture; add more sugar if your fruit is very tart. Keep the marbling effect for presentation; it looks striking in a glass. For a thicker, richer fool, reduce the cream slightly and add extra mascarpone.

Storage

Keep covered in the fridge for up to 2 days. Not suitable for freezing.

Traditional Custard Tarts

Proper English egg custard tarts are scarce in bakeries abroad. You might spot something similar, but it's rarely the real thing. It isn't the silky, nutmeg-dusted classic you'd find on every high street back home. Australian custard tarts are their own thing: denser, more eggy, and often made with a different pastry. But when you're craving the traditional version, creamy and delicate with that unmistakable sprinkle of nutmeg on top, you'll have to make them yourself. One bite and you're right back at a proper British tea table.

Prep Time: 30 minutes
Chill Time: 15 minutes
Total Time: Approx 30 minutes
Cook Time: Approx 1 hour 30 minutes (including chilling)
Makes: 8 individual tarts

Ingredients

For the Pastry
200g plain flour
100g unsalted butter, chilled and cubed
50g icing sugar
1 large egg yolk
1-2 tablespoons cold water

For the Custard Filling
300ml whole milk
200ml double cream
3 large egg yolks
75g caster sugar
1 teaspoon pure vanilla extract
Freshly grated nutmeg to finish

Method

Preheat oven to 160 °C. Sift flour and icing sugar into a bowl. Rub in the butter until the mixture resembles fine breadcrumbs. Stir in egg yolk and add cold water a little at a time until the dough just comes together. Knead lightly, wrap with cling film, and chill for at least 30 minutes.
On a floured surface, roll to 3mm thick. Line tart tins with pastry, trimming any excess. Line with baking parchment and fill with baking beans.
Bake at 160 °C for 15 minutes. Remove baking beans and bake for a further 5 minutes. Allow to cool.
Turn the oven up to 180 °C. Heat milk and cream in a saucepan until steaming. Whisk egg yolks and sugar until pale. Gradually whisk into the hot milk mixture, then stir in vanilla. Pour the custard into the pastry cases. Sprinkle with nutmeg. Bake at 180 °C for 25-30 minutes until set with a slight wobble. Cool before serving.

Adaptations & Substitutions

Pastry: Store-bought shortcrust pastry works well if time is short.
Cream: Substitute double cream with heavy cream if that's what's available.
Sugar: If caster sugar isn't available, use granulated sugar blitzed to a finer consistency. **Spice:** Swap nutmeg for cinnamon or cardamom for a spiced twist. Add citrus zest (orange or lemon) to the custard for brightness.

Tips

For the most fragrant flavour, always add freshly grated nutmeg.
Bake the custards until just set; a little wobble is ideal. Serve warm or cold.

Storage

Keep in the fridge for up to 3 days. Not suitable for freezing.

A Viennetta Style Dessert
A nostalgic delight with layers of ice cream and chocolate

Who could forget the creamy, chocolatey goodness of Walls Viennetta? This homemade version is just as indulgent as the one from the freezer aisle, with the bonus of being made in your own kitchen. Silky vanilla ice cream layered with crisp chocolate makes for a dessert that is both elegant and comforting. Perfect for treating yourself, or impressing friends with a retro classic that never goes out of style. Viennetta is surprisingly simple to make. You just need a little patience because you must freeze each layer of ice cream and chocolate before adding the next. The end result is worth it, a stunning dessert that slices beautifully, tastes nostalgic, and looks impressive on the table.

Prep Time: 30 minutes (hands-on)   **Total Time:** Approx 6½–7 hours   **Makes:** 1 log (8-10 slices)
Freeze Time: At least 6 hours (ideally overnight)

Ingredients

500ml double cream
400ml sweetened condensed milk
1 teaspoon pure vanilla extract
100g dark chocolate
50g butter

Method

Line a 1-litre loaf tin with cling film, leaving an overhang to help lift out the dessert later. Whisk the double cream until it forms soft peaks. Fold in the condensed milk and vanilla until smooth. Spread a layer of the ice cream mixture in the tin. Freeze for 4 hours or until firm.
Melt dark chocolate with butter until smooth. Cool slightly.
Pour a thin layer of melted chocolate over the ice cream.
Freeze for 20-30 minute, until set. Continue layering ice cream and chocolate, freezing in between, until the tin is full.
Freeze the finished dessert for at least 2 hours (or overnight) until completely set. Lift out carefully and remove cling wrap, slice, and serve in generous slabs.

Adaptations & Substitutions

Chocolate: Swap dark chocolate for milk or white chocolate for a sweeter finish. **Flavours:** Add 1 tablespoon of liqueur (Irish Cream, Amaretto, or coffee liqueur) to the ice cream base. **Festive:** Try layering with crushed candy canes or ginger biscuits for a Christmas look. Use single cream whipped with mascarpone instead of double cream for a softer set ice cream.

Tips

Flake extra chocolate on top before serving for texture and visual flair. For fun variations, layer with After Eight mints, orange thins, or coffee thins for added flavour.

Storage

Keeps covered in the freezer for up to 2 weeks. Slice straight from frozen with a sharp knife.

Christmas & Entertaining

> *"Uncle Peter would nod off on the sofa, and we would paint his face with makeup. He would pretend he didn't know. He was such brilliant fun when we were kids. Grandad Barton always sat in the big carver chair that his great-grandad had made, and he would nod off with his apron on and a daft Christmas paper hat on his head."*
>
> —Jane Hardman-Ferris

Christmas began long before sunrise, with the rustle of wrapping paper and Mum calling, "It's too early, go back to sleep." When we finally rushed downstairs to open presents, the turkey was already cooking and the smell of stuffing filled the house.

Mum laid the good tablecloth, set out the best plates and tucked crackers beside each one. The family arrived in a whirl of cold air and laughter, cheeks pink from the winter chill. We squeezed around the table, clinking glasses, passing the gravy boat, groaning at the sprouts and sniggering at the cracker jokes.

After dinner, we lounged with full bellies, our paper crowns crooked and sliding sideways, passing the tin of Quality Street around the room, the Toffee Pennies always left behind. Dad had already drifted off during The Queen's Speech as the fire glowed and the fairy lights twinkled on the tree. A gentle warmth settled over the room like a hug.

I have always loved this season. Mum, though, found it overwhelming. With my birthday just before Christmas, she often said, "I cannot even think about it until I get Linda's birthday out of the way." That was her way of explaining why she never felt ready for the festive chaos.

At Nan's on Boxing Day, one of my favourite treats was homemade pickled onions. One bite instantly transports me to the buffet table. It was makeshift, with cabbage crates as the base and a bedsheet as the cover. There were mini sausage rolls, curling egg sandwiches, and sausages on sticks. A Nat King Cole song crooned in the front room while my cousins and I swayed and giggled, reaching for another Quality Street.

For many of us, Christmas carries both joy and pressure. Shops and TV adverts show us how perfect it should look, and it is easy to feel behind. Yet the heart of Christmas has never been the picture. It lives within those moments of levity, familiar food, plus the tiny traditions of home.

We'll explore planning food for all gatherings, starting with Christmas festivities and quiet events for two. I want to make the season lighter, calmer and full of the warmth it deserves.

Party Food & Tipples

Brie en Croute (That Fancy Cheese Thing From the M&S Ad)
A show-stopping wheel of brie wrapped in golden pastry, perfect for sharing with a glass of bubbles

Festive Slice (UK Bakery Style)
Flaky pastry filled with savoury sausage meat & spiced chutney. A nostalgic nod to the high street bakery.

Goat's Cheese Log with Honey, Fig & Pistachios
A simple but elegant appetiser. Soft cheese meets sweetness and crunch in every bite..

Homemade Herbed Cheese Bites
Soft, creamy morsels rolled in fragrant herbs. Lovely on a grazing board or with crackers.

Mini Yorkies with Rare Roast Beef & Horseradish Cream
Tiny, crisp Yorkshire puddings piled high with tender beef and a punchy cream.

Vol-au-Vents (Classic Chicken & Mushroom, with variations)
No Party table should be without them

Gingerbread
Sweet, spiced, and deeply aromatic. These biscuits bring instant Christmas cheer to any kitchen.

Homemade Sweet Mincemeat
A boozy, spiced filling made ahead to bring mince pies and festive bakes to life.

Mulled Wine or Cider
Fragrant, spiced and warming, this is Christmas in a cup. Perfect for chilly evenings and festive gatherings.

Homemade Irish Cream
Rich, smooth and boozy with a hint of chocolate. Ideal for gifting or pouring over ice after dinner.

Brie en Croute
(That Fancy Cheese Thing From the M&S Ad)

When this first appeared in a Marks & Spencer Christmas advertisement, I knew it had to become part of my festive table. Golden pastry, gooey Brie, and something sweet tucked inside, will look like you've pulled off something posh without trying too hard. A little bit of drama, a lot of taste, and it always disappears first.

Prep Time: 10 minutes
Cook Time: 20–25 minutes
Total Time: 30–35 minutes (plus smugness)
Serves: 6 as a starter or party dish

Ingredients
1 whole round of Brie (250–300 g)
1 sheet puff pastry, thawed
2 tablespoons cranberry sauce or caramelised onion chutney
1 egg, beaten, for glazing
Rosemary sprigs or crushed walnuts, for optional topping

Method
Preheat the oven to 200 °C. Place the Brie in the centre of a sheet of puff pastry. Spoon the cranberry sauce or chutney over the top.
Fold the pastry over to enclose the cheese, pinching to seal. Flip so the seam is underneath.
Place on a baking tray lined with baking paper. For a crisper base, chill for 10 minutes before baking or use a preheated tray.
Brush with beaten egg, sprinkle with rosemary or walnuts if using, and bake for 20–25 minutes, until golden and puffed.
Rest for 5 minutes before cutting to avoid a molten cheese flood.

Adaptions & Substitutions
Swap Brie for Camembert if you prefer a stronger flavour.
Replace cranberry sauce with fig jam (Merry Figgin Christmas Jam recipe in this book), chutney, or relish.
For a savoury twist, use pesto or sun-dried tomatoes.
Add chopped pecans or walnuts inside the pastry parcel for crunch.

Serving Suggestions
Serve warm with sliced baguette, crackers, or crisp apple wedges.
Or place on a wooden board with grapes, herbs, and crackers for a festive centrepiece.
Perfect as a starter, party dish, or part of a Christmas Eve grazing table.

Storage & Reheating
Brie en Croute is best baked fresh and served warm, but you can make it ahead. To store unbaked: Wrap the prepared brie and pastry tightly and keep in the fridge for up to 24 hours.
To freeze: Freeze unbaked, well wrapped. Bake from frozen, adding a little extra time. To store leftovers: Keep cooked Brie en Croute in the fridge for up to 2 days. Reheat gently in the oven until the pastry is crisp and the cheese is soft again. Microwaving turns the pastry soggy.

Festive Slice
(UK Bakery Style)

You can now make at home the festive bake that once drew queues at our bakery. Golden puff pastry holds chicken, stuffing, bacon, cranberries, and creamy white sauce. Forget the turkey and soggy sprouts; this is what people really want. That first creamy, cranberry-filled bite epitomises the celebration of Christmas all wrapped up in flaky pastry. Whether you queued at the high street bakery or are ready to recreate it in your kitchen, this slice delivers festive magic, no drama.

Prep Time: 40 minutes **Total Time:** Approx 1 hour 10 minutes **Makes:** 4 individual festive slices
Cook Time: 25-30 minutes

Ingredients

For the Filling
200g cooked chicken (leftover roast or poached breast), diced
100g sage & onion stuffing (fresh or packet mix)
2 rashers smoked streaky bacon, cooked and chopped
3 tablespoons cranberry sauce (homemade or store-bought)

For the White Sauce
25g butter
25g plain flour
250 ml whole milk Salt, pepper, and a pinch of nutmeg (optional)
2 sheets ready-rolled puff pastry, thawed
1 egg, beaten, for egg wash
Optional: pinch of dried sage or sesame seeds, for topping

Serving Suggestions

Serve warm with salad or roasted vegetables for a light, festive meal.
Perfect as part of a Boxing Day buffet.
Cut into smaller pieces for a party platter or picnic.

Method

Melt the butter in a pan, then stir in the flour to form a roux. Gradually whisk in the milk until thick and smooth. Season with salt, pepper, and nutmeg if using. Set aside the white sauce to cool.
In a bowl, combine the chicken, stuffing, bacon, cranberry sauce, and cooled white sauce until the mixture is thick and spoonable. Cut the pastry sheets into quarters. Arrange on a tray lined with baking paper. Divide the filling onto each square of one sheet of pastry, leaving a border. Brush edges with egg wash. Fold the pastry over the filling, press to seal, and crimp with a fork. Brush tops with egg wash. Score, or sprinkle with sage/sesame seeds if you like.
Bake at 200 °C for 25-30 minutes, until golden and puffed.
Cool slightly before eating. To reheat, warm in a preheated oven at 180 °C for 10-15 minutes to keep the pastry crisp.

Tips

For a bakery-style finish, blitz bread into fine crumbs, toast in a dry pan until golden, cool, and sprinkle over after egg-washing, before baking.

Adaptions & Substitutions

Stuffing: A packet mix works fine, or use the Sage and Onion Stuffing recipe in this chapter. **Chicken:** Leftover roast chicken is perfect. **For a vegetarian version,** swap in mushrooms, roasted vegetables, or plant-based chicken.
Cranberry sauce: Use the supermarket's own or the Cranberry Port and Orange Sauce recipe from this book.

Storage & Reheating

You can store and reheat Festive Slice easily, making it handy for parties or Boxing Day lunches.
To store unbaked: Assemble the parcels, cover, and refrigerate for up to 24 hours. To freeze: Freeze unbaked, well wrapped.
Bake from frozen, adding extra time until golden and piping hot.
To store baked: Keep in the fridge for up to 3 days. Reheat in the oven until warmed through and the pastry is crisp. Avoid microwaving to keep the pastry from going soft.

Goat's Cheese Log
with Honey, Fig & Pistachios

Cheese logs are one of the easiest ways to impress your guests at a gathering. Creamy, tangy, and rolled in nuts and fruit, this version, featuring pistachios, figs, and honey, looks as good as it tastes. Few ingredients, minimal prep, pure perfection.

Prep Time: 15 minutes
Chilling Time: 1–2 hours (overnight is best)

Makes: 1 log to serve 6–8 as an appetiser
Total Time: About 2 hours

Ingredients

200g soft goat's cheese
100g cream cheese
2 dried figs, finely chopped
2 tablespoons honey, plus extra for drizzling
50g pistachios, finely chopped
½ teaspoon cinnamon (optional)
Pinch of salt

Method

In a bowl, mix the goat's cheese, cream cheese, 1 tbsp honey, figs, and salt until smooth. If the mixture is too soft, chill briefly to firm up, then shape into a log. Roll the log in chopped pistachios, pressing lightly to coat.
Wrap in clingfilm and chill for at least 30 minutes, ideally overnight, to allow the flavours to meld and make slicing easier.
Drizzle with extra honey before serving.

Adaptations & Substitutions

Cheese: Swap goat's cheese for ricotta, cream cheese, or brie for a milder flavour. Feta or blue cheese gives a stronger bite.
Nuts: Replace pistachios with walnuts, pecans, almonds, or hazelnuts.
Sweetness: Use maple syrup, fruit preserves, or fig jam instead of honey.
Herbs: Mix in dried thyme, rosemary, or Italian herbs.
Vegan: Use vegan cream cheese or cashew cheese for a dairy-free option.

Serving Suggestions

Slice and serve with crackers, crostini, or crisp apple wedges.
Garnish with fresh fig slices.
Pair with chilled white wine or Prosecco.

Storage

Goat's Cheese Log with Honey, Fig & Pistachios is best served chilled but not straight from the fridge so the flavours shine.
To store assembled: Wrap tightly and refrigerate for up to 3 days.
To make ahead: Roll the cheese log without honey, figs or nuts and chill. Add the toppings just before serving for the best texture.
To freeze: Not recommended, as the texture of the cheese and nuts changes when thawed.

Homemade Herbed
Cheese Bites

These little bites first appeared on our party table after a Christmas food shop with Mum, when we stumbled across Appeteaser cheeses; a small round of soft cheese topped with herbs or spices, made for easy entertaining, just the right size to sit on a small cracker with no cutting or fuss. From then on, no Christmas or family gathering was complete without these tasty morsels. Everyone always loved them piled up beside Ritz crackers, a simple yet special bite. Now, far from home in the UK, and after a few experiments with herbs and spices, they've become that same tradition, creating memories again just as good as the old ones

Prep Time: 20 minutes
Chilling Time: 10-15 minutes
Total Time: 30-35 minutes
Makes: 16-20 pieces (depending on size)

Ingredients

200g cream cheese, or soft goat's cheese
100g feta (for firmer texture and flavour)
1 tablespoon olive oil (optional, for a creamier consistency)
Salt and freshly ground black pepper, to taste

For the Coatings
1 tablespoon dried thyme
1 tablespoon dried basil
1 tablespoon chives, finely chopped
1 tablespoon red pepper flakes, or finely chopped roasted red capsicum (peppers)
1 tablespoon mixed peppercorns, crushed

Method

Combine the cream cheese and feta in a bowl. Mix until smooth, adding olive oil if you prefer a softer texture. Then, season with salt and pepper. Scoop out small portions with a teaspoon. Shape into balls using your hands, two spoons, or a melon baller. A small ice cube tray also works well. Place each coating on separate plates. Roll the cheese bites in thyme, basil, chives, red pepper, or peppercorns to create a variety of flavours. Arrange on a tray and refrigerate for at least 30 minutes until firm.

Adaptations & Substitutions

Cheese: Use ricotta, mascarpone, or blue cheese instead of feta for different textures and flavours.
Herbs & spices: Swap thyme or basil for oregano or dill.
Heat: Use paprika, cayenne, or harissa flakes instead of red pepper flakes.
Crunch: Roll in crushed walnuts, almonds, or sesame seeds for texture.
Vegan: Use plant-based cream cheese and feta alternatives.

Serving Suggestions

Serve chilled with crackers, baguette slices, or olives.
Add grapes or apple slices for sweetness, and scatter almonds or walnuts for crunch. Perfect for a Christmas Eve platter or party spread.

Storage

To store: Place in an airtight container and refrigerate for up to 4 days.
To make ahead: Roll and coat in herbs just before serving keeping them fresh and fragrant.

Mini Yorkies

with Rare Roast Beef & Horseradish Cream

Mini Yorkshire puddings piled with roast beef and a fiery horseradish kick make a show-stealing festive bite your guests won't be able to resist. For best results, serve them straight from the oven. To make hosting stress-free, prepare the batter in advance and store it in the fridge for up to a day. Bake and assemble just before keeping them crisp and delicious.

Cook Time: 20-30 minutes **Total Time:** 50-60 minutes **Makes:** 24 bites
Prep Time: 30 minutes (including batter resting)

Ingredients

For the Yorkshire Puddings
140g plain flour
4 large eggs
200 ml milk
Pinch of salt
Vegetable oil, beef dripping, or butter, for the muffin tin

For the Toppings
300-350g rare roast beef, thinly sliced
150 ml sour cream or crème fraîche
1-2 tablespoons hot horseradish sauce, to taste
Chives or watercress, to garnish (optional)

Method

Whisk the flour, eggs, milk, and salt until smooth. Rest for 30 minutes. Preheat the oven to 220 °C. Add oil or dripping to a mini muffin tin and heat until smoking hot.
Fill each hole with batter just under halfway. Bake for 15-20 minutes until puffed and golden. Do not open the oven early or they won't rise.
Mix the sour cream and horseradish together while the yorkshires cool slightly. Spoon the horseradish cream into each pudding, top with beef slices, and garnish with chives or watercress if desired.

Adaptations & Substitutions

Vegetarian: Replace beef with sautéed mushrooms or roasted veg such as capsicum (peppers) and zucchini (courgette).
Cream: Swap sour cream for Crème fraîche, double cream, or a thick natural yoghurt. **Heat:** Adjust horseradish to taste or use mustard for a gentler kick.

Serving Suggestions

Serve fresh from the oven as a party canapé. Add to a festive platter alongside cheese bites and chutneys. Garnish with micro herbs for a smarter presentation.

Storage & Reheating

To store Yorkshire puddings: Bake ahead, cool completely, and store in an airtight container for up to 2 days. Refresh in a hot oven for a few minutes before serving.
To store assembled: Not recommended, as the puddings will soften. Assemble just before serving.
To freeze: Freeze unfilled Yorkshire puddings for up to 1 month. Reheat from frozen until crisp, then fill with beef and horseradish cream.

Vol-au-Vents

These flaky, buttery pastry cases filled with savoury goodness have, for decades, been a staple at family gatherings, especially at Christmas. Mum made them for parties, and they'd disappear instantly. As an expat, I keep the tradition alive; it brings nostalgia and elegance, even with simple ingredients. Classic flavour defines this version: creamy chicken and mushrooms, comforting and savoury, with a hint of herbs. The filling is rich with butter, cream, and chicken stock, with mushrooms adding earthy depth. The flaky puff pastry gives a light crunch and indulgent texture, making it both homely and a touch fancy. Vol-au-vents, which are both retro and timeless, evoke a nostalgic British charm.

Cook Time: 15 minutes
Prep Time: 20 minutes
Total Time: 35 minutes
Makes: 12–16 small vol-au-vents

Ingredients

Pastry Cases
1 pack puff pastry thawed
1 egg, beaten, for egg wash

Chicken & Mushroom Filling
1 tablespoon butter
1 small onion, finely chopped
1 clove garlic, minced
150g cooked chicken, chopped
100g mushrooms, finely chopped
1 tablespoon plain flour
150 ml chicken stock
2 tablespoons double cream (thickened cream in Australia)
Salt and pepper, to taste
Fresh parsley, chopped (optional)

Serving Suggestion

Serve as part of a festive buffet with pickles, chutneys, and a glass of something bubbly. Perfect for retro-style party platters, sitting alongside sausage rolls and cheese bites.

Method

Make the Pastry Cases
Preheat the oven to 200 °C. Cut 24 circles from the pastry with a 6–8 cm cutter. With a smaller cutter, cut out the centres of half the circles to form rings. Lay the full circles on a baking tray lined with baking paper. Place one ring on top of each base and press down gently. Brush the tops with beaten egg, then add the small cut-out centres to the tray as extra lids or bites. Chill for 15 minutes. Bake for 12–15 minutes until puffed and golden. Cool completely before filling.

Prepare the Filling
Melt the butter in a pan over medium heat. Add onion and garlic, cook until softened. Add mushrooms and cook for 5 minutes. Stir in chicken and flour, cook for 1 minute. Gradually stir in stock, whisking to avoid lumps. Simmer until thick and creamy. Add the cream, season to taste, and stir in the parsley, if using.

Assemble
Spoon the warm filling into cooled pastry cases, taking care not to overfill. For best texture, fill just before serving. If preparing in advance, reheat briefly in a low oven before serving.

Adaptations & Substitutions

Fillings: Swap chicken for ham and cheese, prawns in Marie Rose sauce, roasted vegetables, or spiced lentils. Or select from a choice of fillings from the sandwich filler recipes (Picnics & Sandwiches) in this book.
Herbs: Thyme, tarragon, or dill can replace parsley.

Storage

Bake and cool completely, then keep in an airtight container at room temperature for up to 2 days. To freeze pastry cases: Freeze unfilled cases for up to 1 month. Reheat in a hot oven to crisp before filling. To store filling: Keep the chicken and mushroom mixture in the fridge for up to 2 days. Reheat gently before using. To assemble: Fill just before serving.

Gingerbread

These spiced gingerbread biscuits are a Christmas classic, perfect for hanging on the tree, wrapping as gifts, or enjoying with Irish cream or eggnog. I make stars instead of using chocolate decorations for the tree, since chocolate rarely survives the Australian summer. Dark treacle and ground ginger give a deep, festive flavour. Whether you are trimming the tree or just treating yourself, this gingerbread brings holiday magic.

Prep Time: 20 minutes
Cook Time: 8-10 minutes per tray
Total Time: About 1½ hours (including chilling)
Makes: About 30 biscuits (depending on size of biscuit cutter)

Ingredients

375g plain flour
½ teaspoon ground ginger
½ teaspoon ground cinnamon
½ teaspoon ground cloves
½ teaspoon ground nutmeg
½ teaspoon baking soda
½ teaspoon salt
170g unsalted butter, softened
100g brown sugar, packed
170g dark treacle
1 large egg (about 55 g)
1 teaspoon pure vanilla extract

Method

Mix the flour, ginger, cinnamon, cloves, nutmeg, baking soda, and salt in a medium bowl. In a large bowl, cream the butter and brown sugar until light and fluffy.
Mix in the treacle, egg, and vanilla until the mixture is smooth. Gradually add the dry ingredients until a dough forms. If the mixture is sticky, add a little extra flour. Wrap the dough in clingfilm and refrigerate for at least 1 hour, or overnight. The dough will also firm up during chilling.
Preheat the oven to 180 °C. Line a baking tray with baking parchment. Roll out portions of dough to about 5 mm thick on a lightly floured surface. (see tip)
Cut out shapes with biscuit cutters. (poke a hole if hanging on the tree)
Place biscuits 5 cm apart on the tray. Bake for 8-10 minutes until the edges are golden. Cool on the tray for a few minutes, then transfer to a wire rack to cool completely. Decorate with royal icing or sweets.

Tip

Keep the remaining pastry portions in the fridge until you need them. They soften quickly in the summer heat, and dough that isn't cold becomes sticky and unmanageable quickly.

Serving Suggestions

Serve with mulled wine, hot chocolate, or eggnog. Decorate biscuits with the kids or hang them on the tree as edible ornaments. Store in an airtight container for up to 2 weeks, making them perfect for gifting or preparing ahead.

Storage

Gingerbread keeps beautifully, which makes it perfect for gifting or making ahead. To store baked biscuits: Keep in an airtight container at room temperature for up to 2 weeks. To freeze dough: Wrap well and freeze for up to 3 months. Defrost in the fridge overnight before rolling and baking. To store decorated biscuits: Keep in a cool, dry place for up to 1 week. Avoid humid spots to prevent the icing from softening.

Homemade Sweet Mincemeat

A friend shared this family recipe with me years ago, and I've made it every Christmas since. Rich and spicy, it's perfect for traditional mince pies. Making your own adds a personal touch to festive baking and fills the kitchen with the warm scent of the season. Once you try it, you won't want to go back to shop-bought. It also makes a lovely gift; spoon into a decorative jar, tie with ribbon, and add a handwritten label.

Cook Time: 2–2½ hours (slow oven) 30–40 minutes (stove top)
Prep Time: 10 minutes
Total Time: About 2½–3 hours (slow oven) or 45–55 minutes (stove-top)
Makes: Enough for about 36 mince pies (or fills 2-3 medium jars)

Ingredients

225g cooking apples (or Granny Smiths if cooking apples aren't available), peeled, cored, finely chopped
110g suet
175g raisins
175g sultanas
175g currants
110g mixed peel, chopped
225g soft brown sugar
1 teaspoon ground mixed spice
½ teaspoon ground cinnamon
¼ teaspoon ground nutmeg
Zest and juice of 1 lemon
Zest and juice of 1 orange
50ml brandy, or rum, whisky, or orange juice for an alcohol-free version

Method

Slow-Baked Mincemeat 1. Combine all the ingredients except the brandy in a large mixing bowl. Mix thoroughly. Cover with a clean cloth or clingfilm and leave overnight at room temperature for the flavours to meld. Preheat the oven to 120 °C. Transfer the mixture to a large baking dish, cover loosely with foil, and bake for 2–2½ hours, stirring once or twice. The mixture should darken, become sticky, and smell richly spiced. Remove from the oven and cool for 10–15 minutes. Stir in the brandy while still warm. Spoon into sterilised jars and seal. Store in a cool, dark place for up to 6 months. The flavour improves as it matures.

Quick Stove top Mincemeat

Place all the ingredients except the brandy in a large saucepan. Cook gently over medium–low heat for 25–30 minutes, stirring often, until the fruit is plump and glossy, coated in a thick syrup. Add a splash of juice or water if it looks dry. Cool for 10 minutes, then stir in the brandy while the mixture is still warm. Spoon into sterilised jars, seal, and store as above.

Adaptations & Substitutions

Suet: Use vegetarian suet or grated frozen butter. **Alcohol-free:** Replace brandy with orange or apple juice. **Fruit:** Add or swap in dried cranberries, cherries, or apricots.
Spices: Adjust or add more to taste. **Mixed peel:** If unavailable, use chopped candied orange or lemon slices.

Serving Suggestions

Fill mince pies or festive tarts. Spoon warm over ice cream. Fold into cake or pudding batters. Swirl into yogurt for a festive breakfast. Spread inside puff pastry for quick mincemeat parcels.

Storage

The stove top version is best eaten within 3 months, while the slow-baked version lasts up to 6 months.

Mulled Wine or Cider

Mulled wine is a classic holiday favourite, and while Mum didn't 'do' mulled wine, I think this version is a perfect accompaniment for when you are decorating the tree with friends or enjoying a cosy get-together at Christmas. The warmth of the spices and the rich, fruity flavours make it an ideal drink to sip while sharing laughter and festive memories. If you're feeling nostalgic, mulled wine is a bit like listening to UB40's "Red, Red Wine" at family gatherings - comforting, familiar, and full of cheer. Whether you prefer mulled wine or mulled cider, this spiced drink will add a touch of holiday magic to any occasion.

Cook Time: 15-20 minutes
Prep Time: 5 minutes
Total Time: 20-25 minutes
Makes: About 750 ml mulled wine or about 1 litre mulled cider

Ingredients

- 1 bottle red wine (750 ml), for mulled wine
- 960ml apple cider, for mulled cider or an alcohol-free wine or juice for a non-alcoholic option
- Juice and zest of 1 orange
- 6 cloves
- 3 cinnamon sticks
- 2 star anise
- 1-2 tablespoons honey or sugar, to taste
- ½ teaspoon grated nutmeg (optional)
- 60 ml brandy (optional, for mulled wine)

Method

Combine the wine (or cider), orange zest, and juice in a large pot. Add the cloves, cinnamon sticks, star anise, and honey or sugar. Heat over medium heat, stirring occasionally. Once it steams, reduce the heat and simmer gently for 10-15 minutes. Do not let it boil, as this can affect the flavour and alcohol content. Adjust sweetness to taste. For mulled wine, stir in nutmeg and brandy, then simmer for another 5 minutes. Strain and serve hot, garnished with a cinnamon stick or slice of orange.

Adaptations & Substitutions

Alcohol-free: Use apple juice, cranberry juice, or alcohol-free wine.
Wine: Choose a medium-bodied red, such as Merlot or Shiraz.
Cider: Use still or sparkling cider, adjusting sweetness to taste.
Spices: Add cardamom pods or allspice berries for variation.
Sweetness: Swap honey for maple syrup or golden syrup.

Serving Suggestions

Enjoy with mince pies, gingerbread, or shortbread.
Pair with a cheeseboard — Brie, Camembert, or blue cheese with nuts, olives, and prosciutto.
Serve during tree decorating, on Christmas Eve, or as a warming welcome drink at a party.

Homemade Irish Cream

Mum passed this recipe down to me in the early 1980s, not long after Baileys first appeared in 1974. It's been a family favourite ever since. Rich, creamy, adding a touch of indulgence, and surprisingly easy to make, this liqueur is perfect for sipping, gifting, or sneakily pouring over a dessert.

Prep Time: 10 minutes   **Total Time:** 10 minutes   **Makes:** About 1 litre

Ingredients

300ml single cream (or thickened cream, if single cream isn't available)
170g sweetened condensed milk (about ½ tin)
2 raw eggs (optional, leave out if preferred)
1 tablespoon pure vanilla essence
1 tablespoon instant coffee, or 10ml cooled brewed coffee
3 tablespoons brown sugar
250ml Irish whisky (budget-friendly works fine)

Method

Combine the cream, condensed milk, whisky, coffee, vanilla, sugar, and eggs (if using) in a blender. Blend on low for 30 seconds until smooth.
Pour into a clean glass bottle or jar. Shake well before serving.

Adaptions & Substitutions

Cream: Substitute with coconut cream (300 ml) or use almond/oat milk with plant-based cream.
Condensed milk: Use coconut condensed milk or mix coconut milk with maple syrup until thick and sweet.
Whisky: Swap for rum or bourbon for a unique twist.
Flavourings: Add a few drops of peppermint or almond essence for a festive variation.

Serving Suggestions

With pudding: Pour over a slice of Christmas pudding for an indulgent twist. With chocolate desserts: Serve with truffles, a Yule log, or a chocolate tart. With mince pies: A small glass pairs perfectly with a warm mince pie. With coffee & cake: Use as a boozy creamer in an after-dinner coffee. With cheese: Pair with a cheeseboard; it's especially suited to strong cheddar or blue cheese.

Tips

Adjust creaminess by adding more or less whisky. Taste and tweak the sweetness when using coconut cream, which is naturally rich. Thickened cream in Australia serves as a suitable substitute for single cream. Bottle in a flip-top glass jar, tie with ribbon, and gift as a homemade treat. It's always a winner at Christmas.

Storage

Refrigerate for up to 1 week (or up to 2 weeks without the addition of the eggs if it lasts that long)

Party Food Prep Guide
How much to make, menu planning, drinks planning.

Grazing Boards
Or how to be a Charcutiere Queen

Easy & Impressive Party Food Ideas
Quick canapé/menu inspirations.

Party Food Prep Guide
Be the Hostess with the Mostest (Without Losing Your Mind)

Hosting a party, whether it's for Christmas, a birthday, or just because, can feel overwhelming. You want enough food for everyone without ending up with leftovers for a week (though no judgement if you do). This guide takes the guesswork out of party planning so you can relax and enjoy the occasion without panic.

First, Know Your Guests:

Light eaters or enormous appetites? Kids nibble, adults graze, teenagers devour. Time of day: Afternoon gatherings need lighter options, while evening parties call for more filling bites. Duration: A short gathering needs less. All-night parties call for plenty of nibbles.

How Much to Make?

As a general rule: 8-10 pieces per person for a short drinks party (2 hours). 12-15 pieces per person for a longer party (3-4 hours). 15-20 pieces per person if no meal is being served and the party lasts all evening. Think of it this way: A canapé or bite-sized piece is usually 2-3 bites. People eat more when they're drinking, chatting, and lingering.

Buffet-Style Parties

If you're laying out a buffet rather than trays of canapés, plan for: 150-200g meat or protein per person (cold meats, chicken, fish, vegetarian protein). 100-150g cheese per person, plus crackers or bread. 2-3 side dishes (salads, vegetable platters, dips). 1-2 hot options (pies, vol-au-vents, sausage rolls). Something sweet to finish.

Pro Tips

Make a few vegetarian options and they'll disappear fast, no matter who's at the table. Mix easy shop-bought bites with homemade stars, so you're not tied to the kitchen.

Grazing Boards
(or how to be a Charcuterie Queen)

Let's be honest: anyone can toss cheese and crackers onto a plate. But a true Charcuterie Queen? She turns a grazing board into a work of art, gets people chatting, and watches it disappear faster than you can say "Brie!" Then there are people who improvise when creating their boards, and I am one of them! Whether you're hosting a fancy soiree, treating yourself on a quiet Tuesday, or sneaking one of these delights while watching TV in bed, mastering the grazing board is part creativity, part strategy, and all about fun.

With an eye for balancing colours, textures, and flavours, you'll create spreads where people ask, "How did you think of this?" Ready to dive into the elements that make your grazing board shine? I'm here to help you build boards, step by step, from cheese pairings and flavour combinations to arrangement hacks.

Cheese Pairings, Your Crown Jewels

Every charcuterie queen needs her court, and cheese is top-tier royalty. The trick? Choosing the perfect pairing of sweet with salty, creamy with spicy allows every bite to delight!

Cheese	Fruit Pairing	Something Extra	Drink Match
Brie	Strawberries, figs	Honey, fig jam	Sparkling wine, rosé
Aged cheddar	Apples, grapes	Caramelised onion chutney	Bold red wine, cider
Blue cheese	Pears, dried apricots	Honey, walnuts	Port, dessert wine
Goat cheese	Beets, berries	Pistachios, herb crackers	Sauvignon Blanc
Manchego	Quince paste	Marcona almonds, jamón	Tempranillo, dry sherry

ITEM	QUANTITY PER PERSON
Savoury Bites (e.g. sausage rolls, mini quiches)	4-6 pieces
Skewers (e.g. cheese & pineapple, sausages)	2-3 skewers
Sandwiches (cut small)	2-3 triangles or soldiers
Crisps/chips & dips	1-2 handfuls + dip
Sweets (e.g., cakes, desserts)	2 small portions
Drinks (mix soft & alcoholic)	2-3 per hour

Tip: Overestimate slightly if guests are staying longer or skipping a main meal.

Easy & Impressive Party Food Ideas

Mini Yorkshire Puddings with Roast Beef & Horseradish – a British classic in bite-size form.
Cheese & Onion Rolls – a perfect vegetarian option.
Coronation Chicken Sandwiches – retro and nostalgic.
Pickled Onion Platter – no Christmas table in our house was complete without it.
Trifle Shots – all the joyful layers, served in manageable portions.

Prep Timeline

2-3 Days Before Finalise guest list
Shop for non-perishables
Bake and freeze anything suitable

1 Day Before
Prep sandwiches (cover well)
Slice cheese and meats
Chill drinks

Day of the Party
Assemble cold platters

Serving
Put on your outfit, then relax and
For 12 guests, allow about 18 litres of soft drinks and water, or around 24 bottles of beer, or an equivalent mix.

Drinks Line-Up
Plan for two drinks per guest in the first hour, then one drink per guest, per hour after that.
Warm savoury items just before... Enjoy!

Mini Grazing Cups
The New Party Trick

Charcuterie cups are mini, personal grazing boards that make snacking easy and stylish. Perfect for picnics, barbecues, or any casual get-together.
Fill kraft cups, bamboo cones, or stemless wine glasses for a simple, polished look.

Makes: 1 cup per guest   **Time:** 10 minutes to assemble

What Goes In

Nuts: Pistachios, almonds, or your favourites
Bread: Long crackers or breadsticks for scooping
Olives: Skewered black and green
Meats: Salami, prosciutto, pepperoni
Cheese: Cheddar, Gruyère, Havarti or similar
Fruit: Grapes, berries, apple or peach slices
Herbs: Rosemary, basil or parsley sprigs

Easy Swaps

Vegetarian: Plant-based deli slices, marinated tofu
Gluten-free: GF crackers, flatbreads, rice cakes
Nut-free: Seeds or roasted chickpeas
Fruit & Veg: Seasonal fruit, crudités, cherry tomatoes
Dips: Cream cheese, spinach dip, fondue
Extras: Pickles, chutneys, mustard, hot sauce, flavoured butter

Presentation Tips

Use small bowls for dips and sauces. Keep cheese and fruit central, crackers around the edge. Finish with fresh herbs for a touch of charm. Pre-engraved grazing boards make layout effortless.

Party Menu to Feed 12

Savoury Bites
Mini Sausage Rolls Puff pastry with sausage meat or ground pork and herbs
Cheese & Pineapple Sticks
Classic retro on toothpicks.
Egg Mayo Sandwiches cut into quarters or rolled.
Cocktail Sausages Served hot or cold with mustard dip.
Mini Pork Pies - Homemade or store-bought.
Try mini quiches or small pies with short crust pastry if no mini pork pies.
Pickled Onions (the non-negotiable!) Order from British shops abroad or make your own (see Sauces & Pickles chapter).

Tips

Classic British party foods can be tricky to source abroad, but there are always ways to adapt: Use puff pastry sheets, local cheeses, and chutneys as stand-ins. Include allergy-friendly swaps, such as gluten-free pastry or dairy-free cheese.
Mix shop-bought standbys with homemade favourites to save time.

The Main Event

Christmas dinner isn't just a meal; it's the beating heart of the day, where the golden roast turkey's savoury aroma weaves through crackling laughter and the clink of glasses, drawing everyone back to the table for the feast we wait all year to share.

This chapter brings together the centrepiece dishes and sides that make the meal unforgettable, the recipes that fill the table and the house with warmth. From a tender turkey to crisp sprouts, golden roasties, and rich stuffing, these are the traditions that the family returns to year after year.
And of course, no main event is complete without pudding, whether it's the classic Christmas pudding or a show-stopping Bûche de Noël.

In Perth, Christmas is bloody hot, and the thought of managing the process of a whole roast on the day can feel overwhelming. That doesn't mean we abandon the traditions we grew up with. You could consider scheduling your Christmas roast dinner for the night before and enjoying the traditional dishes on Christmas Eve. The roast, the veg, the trimmings, it's all there, still part of the ritual, simply adjusted to the changing demands of the season.

That leaves Christmas Day itself wide open. You can head to the beach, gather outside, and enjoy a cold platter instead: leftover turkey, glazed ham, cheeses, pickles, and salads. It keeps the spirit of the feast alive while fitting the warmth of a Southern Hemisphere Christmas.

Another trick is to prep ahead. Boil or steam the veg weeks in advance and freeze them.
On the day, you only need to reheat or finish them in the oven with honey, butter, or glaze.
Less time standing over boiling pans in the heat, more oven space for the main event, and much less stress.
Ultimately, it's about adapting without losing the magic, a proper Christmas dinner, the way we remember it, with the freedom to enjoy the sunshine too.

Christmas Prawn Cocktail
Retro, comforting, and always on the table, featuring plump prawns, crisp lettuce, and Marie Rose sauce.

Braised Red Cabbage with Apple
Sweet, tangy, and spiced, with a colour that brightens the Christmas spread.

Honey Roasted Parsnips
Sweet, golden, and caramelised, a Christmas must-have.

Sprouts with Pancetta & Almonds
Brussels sprouts transformed with pancetta, almonds, and a touch of lemon.

Raised Chicken, Bacon & Stuffing Hot Water Crust Pie with Cranberry Top
A towering festive pie with a glossy cranberry crown, packed with chicken, bacon, and stuffing

Pigs in Blankets
The ultimate side or nibble, sausages wrapped in bacon, crisp and irresistible

Roast Turkey British Butcher Style
Shatteringly crispy skin, succulent meat and a bold lemon-garlic butter

Sage & Onion Stuffing
A golden, herby classic with crisp edges and nostalgic flavour.

Traditional Christmas Pudding
Nan's classic, rich, fruity, spiced, and steeped in tradition.

Yule Log (Chocolate Bûche de Noël)
The showstopper, chocolate sponge rolled with cream, finished with fresh fruit.

Christmas Prawn Cocktail

Prawn cocktail is one of those dishes that always makes it onto our Christmas table. There is something comforting about plump, juicy prawns nestled in crisp lettuce with a creamy, tangy Marie Rose sauce. It's retro, it's British, and it always makes me smile. A little nod to tradition that feels just right.

Prep Time: 10 minutes　　**Total Time:** 10 minutes　　**Serves:** 2 as a starter

Ingredients

200g cooked and peeled prawns, rinsed and patted dry (king or tiger prawns work well).
3 tablespoons mayonnaise
1 tablespoon tomato ketchup
1 teaspoon lemon juice
1 teaspoon Worcestershire sauce
Dash of Tabasco or hot sauce (optional)
Freshly ground black pepper
1 small lettuce, shredded
Lemon wedges and paprika, for garnish
Optional: parsley or dill sprigs, for garnish

Method

In a bowl, mix the mayonnaise, ketchup, lemon juice, Worcestershire sauce, and Tabasco, if using. Season with black pepper. Gently fold the prawns into the sauce until evenly coated. Layer shredded lettuce in serving glasses or small bowls. Spoon the prawn mixture over the lettuce. Garnish with a wedge of lemon, a dusting of paprika, and herbs if desired. Serve chilled.

Adaptions & Substitutions

Seafood Swaps: Use shrimp, crab, or lobster. For vegetarians, swap in roasted vegetables.
Lighter Sauce: Replace mayonnaise with Greek yoghurt or use vegan mayonnaise.
Spice: Swap Tabasco for smoked paprika or omit for a gentler flavour.

Serving Suggestions

For the full retro effect, drape a prawn over the rim of the glass. Serve with fresh bread rolls or a crisp green salad. Perfect as a light starter before the Christmas main event.
Make the sauce up to 2 days in advance and store it in the fridge. Stir before using.

Storage

To store sauce: Keep the Marie Rose sauce in an airtight container in the fridge for up to 3 days.
To store prawns: Cooked prawns can be kept in the fridge for up to 2 days. Keep them separate from the sauce.
To assemble: Combine the prawns and sauce just before serving keeping everything fresh and crisp.

Braised Red Cabbage with Apple

Red cabbage isn't the norm on every Christmas table, but it deserves a place. The colour alone looks festive, and when it's braised slowly with apple and spice, it turns into something rich, tangy, and deeply warming. It's the sort of dish you can make a day or two ahead, so there's no stress on the big day. For me, it's the perfect balance to all the richness, cutting through roast potatoes and gravy. It also sits beautifully alongside turkey or ham. And if there's any left over (which is rare in my house), it's wonderful stirred through bubble and squeak on Boxing Day. Choose the oven-baked version if you want to prepare it ahead, or the stove top version for a quicker result.

Prep Time: 15 minutes
Cook Time: (oven): 1 hour 30 minutes **(stove-top):** 30 minutes
Total Time: Varies by method
Serves: 6–8 as a side dish

Ingredients

1 medium red cabbage (about 1 kg), finely shredded
2 large cooking apples, peeled, cored, and grated
1 onion, finely chopped
50g butter
2 tablespoons brown sugar
3 tablespoons red wine vinegar
150 ml apple juice, or water
1 cinnamon stick
2 cloves
Sea salt and freshly ground black pepper

Tips

Make this a day or two ahead. Cool completely, chill, and reheat gently with a splash of extra liquid if needed.

Method

Heat the oven to 160 °C. In a large casserole dish, melt the butter over medium heat. Add the onion and cook until softened. Stir in the cabbage, apple, sugar, vinegar, and apple juice. Add the cinnamon stick and cloves. Season well. 2. Cover tightly with a lid or foil and bake for 1 hour 30 minutes, stirring once or twice. Add a splash more liquid if it looks dry. Remove the spices before serving.

Quick Stove Top Version
Melt the butter in a large pan over medium heat. Add the onion and cook until softened. Stir in the cabbage, apple, sugar, vinegar, and apple juice. Add the cinnamon stick and season. Cover and cook gently for 25–30 minutes, stirring occasionally, until the vegetables are tender but still bright. Add a splash more liquid if it looks dry. Remove the cinnamon stick before serving.

Serving Suggestions

Serve hot alongside turkey, ham, or glazed pork. The sweet-sour flavour also balances rich dishes like goose, duck, or a hearty vegetarian nut roast. Leftovers are perfect stirred into bubble and squeak on Boxing Day.

Storage & Reheating

Braised Red Cabbage with Apple keeps beautifully and actually improves in flavour after a day or two.
To store: Cool and refrigerate in an airtight container for up to 5 days.
To freeze: Freeze for up to 3 months. Defrost in the fridge overnight.
To reheat: Warm gently in a pan or oven, adding a splash of water or cider vinegar to loosen if needed.

Honey Roasted Parsnips

Parsnips are one of my favourite vegetables. Sweet and delicious, they're a must on the Christmas dinner plate. There's something about them that feels festive, almost as if they've been waiting all year for this moment of glory. Roasted until caramelised, with golden edges and just enough honey to draw out their natural sweetness, they're the side dish I always look forward to most. Sweet, caramelised parsnips with crisp edges, the perfect match for roast potatoes and gravy.

Prep Time: 10 minutes
Cook Time: 40 minutes

Total Time: 50 minutes

Serves: 6 as a side dish

Ingredients

1kg parsnips, peeled and halved or quartered lengthwise (depending on size).
2 tablespoons olive oil
2 tablespoons honey
1 tablespoon wholegrain mustard (optional)
Sea salt and freshly ground black pepper

Method

Heat the oven to 200 °C. Bring a pan of salted water to the boil. Add the parsnips and cook for 3-4 minutes until just tender. Drain well. Tip the parsnips into a roasting tin. Drizzle with oil, honey, and mustard, if using. Season and toss to coat.
Roast for 30-35 minutes, turning once, until golden and caramelised.

Serving Suggestions

Serve hot alongside roast turkey, beef, or ham, with plenty of gravy. They also pair beautifully with nut roasts for a vegetarian main.

Tips

Parboil and coat the parsnips earlier in the day and store covered in the fridge. Roast just before serving.

Storage

Keep cooked parsnips in an airtight container in the fridge for up to 3 days.
To freeze: Freeze roasted parsnips for up to 1 month. Reheat from frozen or thaw overnight in the fridge.
To reheat: Warm in a hot oven until golden and sticky.
Add a touch more honey just before serving if needed.

Brussels Sprouts with
Pancetta & Almonds

Ah, Brussels sprouts, a Christmas tradition with a mixed reputation, can be a showstopper when prepared well. Roast them with olive oil and sea salt, sauté them with pancetta, or toss them with roasted chestnuts, and they transform from dreaded to devoured. Cooked until just tender, with a bit of bite, and paired with bacon, pancetta, or almonds, sprouts suddenly become the star of the table. For a vegetarian twist, swap the pancetta for sliced mushrooms or add a sprinkle of smoked paprika.

Prep Time: 5 minutes **Total Time:** 20 minutes **Serves:** 4 as a side dish
Cook Time: 15 minutes

Ingredients

500g Brussels sprouts, trimmed and halved
100g pancetta, diced
70g flaked almonds
1 tablespoon olive oil
1 tablespoon butter
Sea salt and freshly ground black pepper
Zest of 1 lemon (optional, for freshness)

Method

Heat the olive oil and butter in a large frying pan over medium heat.
Add the pancetta and cook for about 5 minutes, stirring occasionally, until crisp.
Add the Brussels sprouts, cut side down. Cook for 5–7 minutes, turning occasionally, until golden on the cut side and just tender inside.
Toast the almonds in a separate dry pan for 3–4 minutes, stirring often, until they are golden. Toss the almonds, sprouts and pancetta.
Sprinkle with lemon zest, if using. Season with salt and pepper.
Serve hot, letting guests enjoy the crispy texture and rich flavour.

Serving Suggestion

Perfect with roast turkey or ham, or as a side dish to vegetarian mains. For a British touch, pair with roast potatoes and gravy. Left overs are delicious stirred into bubble and squeak the next day.

Storage & Reheating

To store: Keep cooked sprouts with pancetta in the fridge for up to 2 days.
To prep ahead: Blanch the sprouts earlier in the day, then fry with pancetta just before serving for the best texture.
To reheat: Warm gently in a frying pan to keep the pancetta crisp.
To freeze: Not recommended, as the sprouts can turn soft and watery once thawed.

Raised Chicken, Bacon & Stuffing Hot Water Crust Pie
with Cranberry Top

In the run-up to Christmas, I always remember the Sainsbury's supermarket deli counter. I salivated over their magnificent pies every December. They were a proper showstopper, a genuine love letter to British pie-making. Among the stuffed olives and peppercorn-crusted hams, the pies loomed tall and proud. Their pastry shimmered, topped with glistening cranberry jewels. So, this is the pie I make instead. Same impressive stance, same glossy cranberry crown, but filled with the good stuff: chicken, smoky bacon, and herby stuffing. It's a pie that looks the part, tastes of Christmas, and vanishes fast once the first slice is served

Prep Time: 45 minutes
Cook Time: 1 hour 30 minutes
Total Time: about 3 hours 15 minutes
Resting Time: 10–15 minutes
Serves: 8 as a main

Ingredients

For the pastry
600g plain flour
150g lard, chopped
150g butter, chopped
1 teaspoon salt
200 ml water

For the Filling
600g skinless chicken thighs, cut into 1" chunks
200g smoked streaky bacon, chopped
200g pork sausage meat, or skinned sausages
1 onion, finely chopped
2 garlic cloves, crushed
2 teaspoons dried sage
2 teaspoons dried thyme
100g fresh white breadcrumbs
1 egg, beaten (for binding)
Sea salt and freshly ground black pepper

To Finish
1 egg, beaten (for glazing)
200g cranberry sauce

Method

Heat the oven to 180 °C. Grease and line with baking parchment a 20 cm deep springform tin. Put the flour and salt in a large bowl. In a pan, melt the lard, butter, and water until just boiling. Pour the hot mixture into the flour, stir with a wooden spoon, then knead until smooth. Wrap in cling wrap and keep warm while you prepare the filling.

Prepare the Filling

In a frying pan, cook the bacon until lightly crisp. Add the onion and garlic and cook until softened. Leave to cool slightly. In a bowl, combine the chicken, sausage meat, bacon mixture, herbs, breadcrumbs, and beaten egg. Season generously.

Roll out two-thirds of the pastry approximately 5mm thick and line the tin, pressing into the corners and leaving some overhang. Fill with the meat mixture, pressing down well. Roll out the remaining pastry for a lid. Brush the edges with egg, seal with a fork, trim, and crimp. Cut a steam hole in the centre. Brush with egg wash and bake for 1 hour 15 minutes until golden. Ensure the filling reaches an internal temperature of at least 75 °C. Cool the pie in the tin for 30 minutes, then carefully remove it. Once the pie is cold, spoon the cranberry sauce over the top.

Raised Chicken, Bacon & Stuffing Hot Water Crust Pie
with Cranberry Top

Tip
If you can't find British-style sausage meat, use skinned local sausages and mash the filling until smooth. Pork, chicken, or turkey sausages all work well).(see Cranberry, Port & Orange sauce in the Sauces & Pickles chapter)

Adaptations & Substitutions
Cranberries: If cranberry sauce isn't available, try lingonberries, redcurrants, or tart cherry jam. Or adapt the Cranberry Sauce recipe from this book. **Pastry fats:** If lard is unavailable, replace with butter or vegetable shortening.

Serving Suggestions
Serve warm or at room temperature. Pair with buttery mash, roasted sprouts, or a crisp green salad. A jug of gravy on the side makes it extra comforting.

Storage
Keep in the fridge for up to 4 days. Wrap and freeze for up to 3 months. Defrost in the fridge over night.

Pigs in Blankets

I've always enjoyed pigs in blankets, not just at Christmas but anytime there's a feast to share. Their simple combination of sausages and crispy bacon brings back memories of family gatherings and good cheer. My special touch is to serve them with a tangy mustard dip or arrange them elegantly on a platter with sprigs of rosemary and cranberries, making every gathering feel extra festive and inviting.

Prep Time: 10 minutes
Cook Time: 20–25 minutes
Total Time: 25 minutes
Serves: 12 as a side dish

Ingredients
12 British sausages (or local varieties such as Italian or chorizo for extra flavour)
12 rashers unsmoked streaky bacon
1 tablespoon maple syrup or honey (optional, for sweetness)
Freshly ground black pepper, to taste

Method
Preheat the oven to 200 °C. Lay each bacon rasher flat, place a sausage at one edge, and roll tightly. Arrange on a parchment-lined baking tray, spacing them apart for even cooking. Drizzle with maple syrup or honey, if using, and season with black pepper. Roast for 20–25 minutes, until the bacon turns golden and the sausages cook through. (The juices should run clear when skewered, or check they've reached an internal temperature of 72 °C.)

Adaptations & Substitutions
Posh Pigs: Swap the bacon for prosciutto or pancetta, wrap around cocktail sausages, and brush with a mix of honey and wholegrain mustard before roasting. They'll cook in 15–20 minutes and come out crisp and sticky. **Bacon:** Try pancetta, prosciutto, or even home-cured bacon (see our Homemade British Back Bacon recipe in the Butcher The Baker The Breakfast Maker chapter of this book).
Sausages: Use turkey, chicken, plant-based sausages, or local varieties instead of traditional bangers. **Sweetness:** Maple syrup, honey, or brown sugar will add a caramelised glaze, but you can leave them plain.

Serving Suggestions
Pile onto a platter with rosemary sprigs for garnish. Serve with mustard, cranberry sauce, or chutney for dipping. Perfect as part of a roast dinner, on a festive platter, or as a hot snack.

Storage & Reheating
To store uncooked: Assemble and refrigerate on a tray, covered, for up to 2 days. To freeze uncooked: Freeze on a tray, then transfer to a container or bag. Cook from frozen, adding extra time.
To store cooked: Keep in the fridge for up to 3 days.
To reheat: Warm in a hot oven until sizzling and crisp. Avoid microwaving as it softens the bacon.

Roast Turkey, British Butcher Style
With Lemon, Garlic Butter & Pan Gravy

This roast get sits flavour not from stuffing, but from aromatics in the cavity, a bold lemon-garlic butter under the skin, and plenty of basting. My British butcher friend, Steve Patterson, taught me this approach, and the result is shatteringly crisp skin, succulent meat, and gravy that makes the whole roast worth the wait.

Prep Time: 25 minutes **Serves:** 8–10
Cooking Time: 30 minutes per kilo, plus resting

Ingredients

For the Turkey
- 1 whole turkey, giblets removed
- 2 mandarins, halved
- 2 lemons, halved (plus zest and juice of 1 for the butter)
- 2 brown onions, halved
- 3–4 sprigs fresh rosemary
- 3–4 sprigs fresh thyme
- Salt and freshly cracked black pepper

For the Lemon & Garlic Butter
- 300g unsalted butter, softened
- 2 tablespoons mild olive oil
- 2 cloves garlic, crushed
- Zest and juice of 1 lemon
- 2 tablespoons fresh flat-leaf parsley, finely chopped
- Salt and freshly cracked black pepper

For the Gravy
- Roasting juices and fat from the turkey tin
- Fruit, onions, and herbs from the cavity, chopped.
- 1–2 rashers of bacon, cooked and chopped (optional)
- 2 tablespoons plain flour
- 500ml chicken or vegetable stock
- A splash of vegetable cooking water (optional)
- Salt & freshly ground black pepper

Method

Cooking the Turkey

Preheat the oven to 220°C. Season the cavity with salt and freshly ground black pepper.
Cut the mandarins, lemons, and onions in half and place them inside the turkey with the rosemary and thyme.

Mix the butter, oil, garlic, lemon zest and juice, parsley, salt, and pepper. Gently slide your fingers under the breast skin and spread half of the butter mixture evenly over the breast meat.
Repeat from the neck end, then rub the remaining butter over the outside of the bird. Season the skin.

Loosely tie the legs with kitchen string to hold the fruit and herbs in place, then place the turkey breast-up in a roasting tin.
Roast for approximately 2½ hours (30 minutes per kilo) at 180°C.
Start by roasting at 220°C for 10–15 minutes to crisp the skin, then reduce to 180°C.

Baste the turkey with the juices every 30 minutes to ensure it remains moist and flavourful.
To cook the turkey thoroughly and safely, use a meat thermometer and check the thickest part reaches 74°C.
Remove the turkey from the roasting tin and transfer to a platter.
Rest it loosely covered with foil for at least 30-60 minutes, or ideally for the same time as it has cooked.

Roast Turkey, British Butcher Style
With Lemon, Garlic Butter & Pan Gravy

Make the Gravy

Drain most of the fat from the roasting tin, keeping 2–3 tbsp for flavour. Place the tin over medium heat.

Mash the fruit, onions, herbs and bacon (if using) add to the tin. Mashing lightly with a fork releases their flavour.

Stir in the flour and cook for 1–2 minutes. Gradually add the stock and a splash of vegetable water, scraping up all the caramelised bits from the tin.

Simmer for 5–10 minutes until glossy and thickened.

Season to taste, and strain if you prefer a smooth finish.

Carve and serve with roast potatoes, stuffing, and a generous helping of gravy.

Tips

Roasting the turkey for 2½ hours and resting it for the same time brings out more juiciness and flavour. A longer rest also gives you time to make the gravy, ensuring the turkey remains moist and easy to carve. And the best tip from Steve is, "If you think you've basted it too many times, do it some more!

Storage & Reheating

To store uncooked: Prepare the turkey (stuffed or unstuffed), cover, and refrigerate for up to 1 day before roasting.

To store cooked: Cool quickly, then refrigerate for up to 3 days.

Slice off the breast meat to store separately for easier reheating.

To freeze: Freeze cooked turkey for up to 3 months. Defrost in the fridge overnight.

To reheat: Cover with foil and warm gently in the oven with a splash of stock or butter to keep it moist.

Avoid overcooking.

Braised Red Cabbage with Apple

Sage & Onion Stuffing

Sage & Onion Stuffing

Homemade sage and onion stuffing was always Mum's specialty to accompany her roast chicken on a Saturday lunchtime, no shortcuts, just day-old breadcrumbs, butter, and, when possible, fresh herbs. The simple mix of onions, sage, thyme, and breadcrumbs, all combined with melted butter, became something special in her hands. I prefer baking it separately for crisp golden edges. Mum always said it was the reason people returned to ask for seconds. This recipe pays homage to my mum's legendary roast dinners, which deserve the made-from-scratch love. Prepare ahead and freeze for busy days: shape and cook, then cool and freeze in an airtight container. Reheat when needed to enjoy fresh flavours.

Prep Time: 10 minutes
Cook Time: 30–35 minutes
Total Time: 40 minutes
Serves: 6–8 as an accompaniment

Ingredients

250g bread
(1–2 days old works best; white, wholemeal, or sourdough for different textures and flavours)
2 large white onions, finely diced
2 tablespoons fresh sage, finely chopped
1 teaspoon fresh thyme, finely chopped
¼ teaspoon each salt and black pepper
50g unsalted butter
Canola or olive oil spray, as needed
Optional add-ins: minced garlic
sausage meat, dried or fresh cranberries, chestnuts
Orange or lemon zest

Method

Preheat the oven to 180°C. Blitz the bread into coarse breadcrumbs in a food processor and set aside.
Add the diced onions to a pan with just enough water to cover. Boil gently until soft. Remove from the heat. Add the herbs, breadcrumbs, salt, and pepper, and stir. Add a splash of water if the mixture feels dry.
Mix in garlic or sausage meat at this stage, if using. Fold in cranberries, chestnuts, or zest at the end, if you'd like. Spray a baking dish with oil, add the stuffing, and level the top. Dot with butter and bake for 30–35 minutes until crisp and golden brown. Let rest for a few minutes before serving.

Serving Suggestions

Serve with roast turkey, chicken, or pork. Pair with a nut roast for a vegetarian feast. A spoonful of gravy over the top makes it extra comforting. Leftovers are brilliant cold in sandwiches the next day, especially with cranberry sauce.

Tips

Stuffing helps keep the turkey moist if used in the cavity. Fill lightly and never pack tightly. Shape into golf ball-sized portions and bake alongside roast potatoes. Freeze-dried sage and thyme can replace fresh herbs if needed.

Storage & Reheating

To store uncooked: Keep covered in the fridge for up to 2 days before baking. To freeze uncooked: Freeze for up to 1 month. Defrost in the fridge overnight, then bake as usual.
To store cooked: Refrigerate in an airtight container for up to 3 days.
To reheat: Warm in the oven, covered with foil, until piping hot. Uncover for the last few minutes to crisp the top.

Traditional Christmas Pudding

This is my Nan's Christmas pudding recipe. I took over cooking it just after she passed away in 1988. I haven't changed it, not just because it is delicious, but because I'm fairly sure she would haunt me if I tried to meddle with it. Every year, she would tuck a sixpence or a lucky charm into the pudding. As children, we would fight to find it (or nearly break a tooth). I still have a tiny silver duck, tarnished with age but priceless to me. It's a small reminder of big family traditions, laughter, and generous dollops of custard. We always had custard, because Nan's brandy butter was so heavy on the brandy that one spoonful could set your eyelashes on fire. Delicious, yes, but definitely not child-friendly.

Prep Time: 30 minutes (plus overnight soaking)

Cook Time: 6–8 hours (first steam)

Resting Time: Ideally 4–6 weeks

Makes: 4 small puddings (450 ml basins, 2 servings each), 3 medium puddings (750 ml basins, 3 servings each), or 1 large pudding (1250 ml basin, 8 servings)

Reheat Time (on Christmas Day): 2 hours steaming

Ingredients

200g self-raising flour
½ teaspoon salt
1 teaspoon cinnamon
1 teaspoon nutmeg
1 teaspoon ground mixed spice
200g breadcrumbs
200g shredded suet Juice and rind of 1 orange
200g raisins
200g currants
200g sultanas
100g mixed peel
150g demerara sugar
1 apple, grated
4 eggs, beaten
100 ml brandy
200 ml milk, stout, or ale

Method

Overnight Soak
Place the raisins, currants, sultanas, and mixed peel in a large bowl.
Add the orange juice and zest, brandy, and stout (or ale/milk if using).
Stir well, cover with a tea towel, and leave to soak overnight.

Sieve the flour, salt, and spices into a large bowl.
Stir in the breadcrumbs, suet, sugar, and grated apple.
Add the soaked fruit (with all the liquid) and the beaten eggs.
Mix thoroughly; it should be a soft, spoonable consistency.

Spoon into greased pudding basins, leaving 1 cm at the top. Cover the basin with a layer of baking parchment topped with foil, both pleated in the centre to allow for rising. Secure tightly around the rim with string, then fold the overhanging edges upwards so they don't dip into the water.
For easier lifting, tie another length of string across the top to form a handle.
Place the basins into a large pan. Pour in boiling water until it reaches two-thirds of the way up the sides. Boil gently for 8 hours, topping up with boiling water as needed, or steam for 10 hours.
Cool completely.
On Christmas Day, reheat by boiling or steaming for 2–3 hours.
Serve hot with brandy butter, cream, or custard for a safer option for children.

Traditional Christmas Pudding

Tips

Suet abroad: Use vegetable suet or grate frozen butter if unavailable. In Australia, Coles and Woolworths sell Tandaco suet, which works perfectly well. **Mixed spice:** Make your own with cinnamon, nutmeg, and allspice.
Dried fruit: Some brands label currants and sultanas differently. (e.g. raisins, golden raisins). **Overnight soak:** Don't skip this step; it plumps the fruit, balances the spices, and gives the pudding its rich, moist texture. Replace the covers with fresh ones (foil or calico works well), then store in a cool, dry place. Well wrapped, the pudding will keep for up to 6 months.
Cream: If double cream is unavailable, use thickened or heavy cream as a substitute.

Storage & Reheating

To store cooked pudding: Wrap tightly and keep in a cool, dark cupboard for up to 3 months, or refrigerate for the same period. Feed the pudding with a little extra brandy or rum during storage to keep it rich and moist.
To freeze: Wrap well and freeze for up to 1 year. Defrost in the fridge overnight before reheating.
To reheat: Steam for 1 hour or microwave individual portions until piping hot.

Yule Log
(Chocolate Bûche de Noël)

Yule Log was always the "Ta Da" dessert on our Christmas table, rich and chocolatey, with a touch of magic in its log-like swirl and dusting of snow. We usually picked it up from Iceland (the supermarket, not the country), and while Christmas pudding was for the grown-ups, this was the kids' favourite (and secretly the adults' too). Sometimes, I didn't bake the sponge from scratch; I'd grab a supermarket chocolate swiss roll, unroll it, spread buttercream, re-roll it, and cover it with icing. Done. Festive magic, no complaints, and gone in minutes.

These days, I make the sponge myself, but honestly, both bring the same joy.

It looks impressive, but it's easier than it seems. Whether homemade or refreshed from store-bought, it's always a crowd-pleaser.

Prep time: 25–30 minutes

Cook time: 10–12 minutes

Total time: 40–45 minutes (plus cooling/chilling)

Makes: 1 sponge roll

Ingredients

For the Sponge
4 large eggs
100g caster sugar
65g plain flour
40g cocoa powder (unsweetened)
1 teaspoon pure vanilla extract
Pinch of salt

For the Filling
150ml double cream (heavy or thickened cream)
1 tablespoon icing sugar (powdered sugar)
1 teaspoon vanilla extract

For the Ganache Topping
100g dark chocolate (I use normal, not cooking chocolate)
100ml double cream (heavy cream)
1 teaspoon golden syrup or honey (optional, for shine)

Method

Preheat oven to 180°C. Line a Swiss roll tin or shallow tray (23 × 33 cm) with baking parchment.

Whisk eggs and sugar with a mixer until thick, pale, and ribbon-like.

Sift flour, cocoa, and salt, then fold gently into the egg mixture with vanilla.

Spread evenly on the tin. Bake 10–12 minutes, until the sponge springs back when lightly pressed.

Lay a clean tea towel on the bench and dust it with icing sugar.

Turn the warm sponge onto it, peel off the paper, and roll up from the short end with the towel inside. Leave rolled to cool completely.

Whip cream, icing sugar, and vanilla to soft peaks.

Unroll the sponge, spread it with cream, and then re-roll it without the towel.

Place seam-side down. Chill 10–15 minutes to set.

Ganache topping Heat cream until steaming. Pour over chocolate, rest for 2 minutes,
then stir until smooth. Add syrup if using. Cool until spreadable. Cover the sponge generously. Drag a fork through for bark effect.

Decorate
Dust with icing sugar "snow" or garnish with holly, berries, or marshmallow mushrooms.

RECIPE CONTINUED ON NEXT PAGE...

Yule Log
(Chocolate Bûche de Noël)

Adaptations & Substitutions

Add a splash of brandy or orange liqueur to the filling or sponge. For non-alcoholic, try orange zest or extract. **Allergy-Friendly Dairy-free:** Use plant cream and dairy-free chocolate. **Gluten-free:** Swap plain flour for a baking-ready GF blend. **No caster sugar?** Blitz granulated sugar briefly for a finer texture. **No Swiss roll tin?** Use a shallow tray and trim the edges. Don't panic about cracks; ganache covers all, and they even add bark-like charm.

Serving Suggestions

Slice and serve with cream or ice cream. Perfect with tea or mulled wine. Keeps 3–4 days in the fridge or up to 1 month frozen (thaw overnight in the fridge).

Storage

Keep in the fridge, covered, for up to 3 days. Store sponge only: Bake and roll the sponge, then wrap tightly and store at room temperature for 1 day or freeze for up to 1 month. Freeze assembled: Not ideal, as the cream can split, but you can freeze without icing and decorate after thawing. Thaw overnight in the fridge. Bring to room temperature before serving for the best texture.

Eating In Like You're Eating Out

Recreating a Restaurant Experience at Home

Flame Grilled Burger

Recreating a Restaurant Experience at Home

Ah, good old Marks & Spencer. Home of the "Meal for Two" and those restaurant-quality dinners that made any evening feel special. We saved ours for Friday Date Night, when Carl would stop by M&S on his way home.
Fridays became our time to unwind, phones off, enjoying a meal together and reminding ourselves to stay connected. These days, I still like to make an occasion of it. I'll set the table with our posh plates, light a few candles and pour something nice into the wedding-gift glasses. Small rituals like that remind us to slow down and savour time together.

Eating In Like You're Eating Out is about bringing that same feeling home, turning an ordinary evening into something quietly special. It isn't about complicated cooking or fancy ingredients; it's about good food, a little care, and the people you share it with.

Even the simplest meal feels different when you serve it beautifully. Use your nicest plates, scatter a few herbs, and take a moment to make it look lovely. Add a small flourish, maybe a drizzle of truffle oil, a few prawns tossed through the sauce, or something new you haven't tried before. Give each dish a bit of time to shine: let the chicken turn golden, the vegetables stay tender, and the sauce reduce until it's just right. Pour a glass of wine, light a candle, and put on some music. A relaxed atmosphere and a little patience can turn a night in into a night out.

So, whether it's a pub classic, a bistro-style dish or a curry-night favourite, these recipes will help you bring the restaurant experience to your own table, warm, comforting and made with love.
With just a few good ingredients and a little time, you can create delicious, satisfying meals that are still easy to prepare. No fancy skills needed, just follow some simple steps, enjoy the process, and make your meals feel a bit more special.

Pub Classics

Proper Dinners, Done Right

Here's to proper food — the sort you'd order at a pub back home, only made better because you've done it yourself. Think golden batter, rich gravies, suet puddings and roast joints that make the kitchen smell like Sunday. These are the meals that fill the house with warmth and make a night in feel like a treat out.

Proper Fish & Chips

Golden battered fish with chunky chips and chip-shop curry sauce, complete with scraps for that true seaside feel.

Steak & Kidney Pudding

A suet-crusted classic with a splash of stout. Hearty, nostalgic, and pure comfort.

Stuffed Roast Pork Loin

A clever way to stretch a small joint, butterflied and filled with herby stuffing, perfect for a Sunday-style dinner any night.

Yorkshire Puddings Two Ways

Crisp on the outside, soft inside. Serve as traditional puds or turn them into wraps filled with roast beef or sausages and gravy.

Proper Fish & Chips
with Chip Shop Curry Sauce (and Scraps)

Nothing quite hits the spot like proper British fish and chips: with their golden, crispy batter, fluffy thick-cut chips, and that unmistakable hit of salt and vinegar. Whether eaten straight from the paper wrapping at the seaside or as a comforting chippy tea at home, this dish is pure nostalgia for expats. Recreate the real deal with this classic recipe and don't forget the mushy peas and a good drizzle of malt vinegar.

Prep Time: 15 minutes **Cook Time:** 30 minutes **Serves:** 4 as a main dish
Total Time: 45 minutes

Ingredients

For the Fish
4 boneless white fish fillets (cod, haddock, snapper or basa)
100g plain flour, for dusting
Salt and pepper
Sunflower or vegetable oil for frying

For the Batter
150g plain flour
1 teaspoon baking powder
1 teaspoon salt
200ml cold sparkling water or beer

For the Chips
4 large floury potatoes (e.g. Nadine, Sebbago, Coliban.
Oil, for frying
Salt, to serve

Optional Sides
Mushy peas
Malt vinegar or substitute
Lemon wedges

For Chip Shop Curry Sauce
1 tablespoon vegetable oil
1 onion, finely chopped
1 garlic clove, minced
1 tablespoon curry powder
1 tablespoon plain flour
250ml vegetable stock
1 tablespoon tomato ketchup
1 teaspoon soy sauce

Method

Prepare the Chips 1. Peel and cut the potatoes into thick chips. Rinse and parboil for 5 minutes. Drain and dry briefly.

First Fry
Heat oil to 140 °C Fry chips in batches for 5–7 minutes until pale and soft. Drain onto kitchen paper.

Make the Batter
Mix flour, baking powder, and salt. Whisk in cold sparkling water or beer to form a thick batter. Rest for 10 minutes.

Fry the Fish
Heat oil to 180 °C Pat fish dry, season with salt and pepper, dust with flour, dip in batter, and fry for 6–8 minutes until golden. Drain well.

Second Fry (Chips)
Reheat oil to 180 °C Fry chips for 2–3 minutes until crisp and golden. Drain and season with salt.

Chip Shop Curry Sauce
Heat oil in a pan over medium heat. Sauté onion and garlic for 3-4 minutes until soft. Stir in curry powder and flour, cooking for 1 minute.

RECIPE CONTINUED ON NEXT PAGE ...

Proper Fish & Chips
with Chip Shop Curry Sauce (and Scraps)

Add stock, ketchup, and soy sauce. Simmer for 5–10 minutes until thickened. Season with salt and pepper to taste.

Scraps / Batter Bits
Skim any leftover crispy batter bits from the oil, drain on kitchenpaper, and serve alongside the fish and chips.

Tips

Fish options: If cod or haddock aren't available, snapper, basa, barramundi, or pollock work well. Choose firm, boneless fillets.
Beer vs sparkling water: Beer gives a richer batter; sparkling water makes it lighter.
No fryer? Use a deep saucepan with a thermometer.

Fry safely and never leave unattended.

Serving Suggestions

Pile on to a plate (or wrap in butcher's paper for the full effect) with mushy peas, pickled onions, and a splash of malt vinegar.

Storage & Reheating

Fish: Store cooled fillets in an air tight container in the fridge for up to 2 days. Reheat in a preheated oven at 180 °C for 10–12 minutes until hot and crisp. Avoid microwaving, as the batter will turn soggy.

Chips: Best eaten fresh. If you must store them, keep in the fridge for up to 2 days. Reheat on a baking tray at 200 °C for 8–10 minutes until hot and crisp.

Curry sauce: Store in an airtight container in the fridge for up to 3 days or freeze for up to 2 months. Reheat gently on the stove, adding a splash of water if needed.

Steak & Kidney Pudding

Nan always kept a bottle of stout tucked away in the sideboard, along side the mismatched china and a tin of peaches ready for emergency puddings. A splash of that stout turns a good steak and kidney pudding into something unforgettable, giving it depth, comfort and a touch of nostalgia.

Prep Time: 30 minutes **Cook Time:** 2½–3 hours **Serves:** 4–6 as a main dish
Total Time: 3–3½ hours

Ingredients

For the Filling
500g beef steak, chopped into small cubes
250g lamb's kidneys washed, trimmed and chopped
1 large onion, finely chopped
2 tablespoon plain flour
2 tablespoon vegetable oil
1 teaspoon Worcestershire sauce
250ml stout (dark, such as Guinness or Murphy's)
250ml beef stock
1 teaspoon dried thyme
Sea salt and freshly ground black pepper

For the Suet Pastry
250g self-raising flour
125g suet (or 125 g chilled unsalted butter)
1 teaspoon salt
150 ml cold water

Method

Make the Pastry
In a large bowl, combine flour, suet (or chilled unsalted butter) and salt. Gradually add cold water, stirring until a soft dough forms. Turn onto a floured surface and knead gently until smooth. Wrap with clingfilm and set aside.

Prepare the Filling
Heat oil in a large pan over medium heat. Add onion and cook until softened. Add beef and kidney, browning the meat on all sides.
Sprinkle in flour, stir to coat, and cook for 1–2 minutes.
Add stout, beef stock, Worcestershire sauce and thyme. Stir and bring to a simmer. Season with salt and pepper, cook gently for 30 minutes, until the meat is tender and the sauce has thickened

Assemble and steam the pudding
Grease a pudding basin with oil or butter. Roll out two-thirds of the pastry about 5mm thick to line the basin, reserving the rest for the top. Spoon in the filling, then roll out the remaining pastry.
Cover, seal the edges with a fork and trim the excess. Cover basin with baking parchment or foil, securing tightly with kitchen string if needed. Place in a large pot of simmering water (halfway up the sides of the pudding basin). Cover with a lid and steam for 2–2½ hours, topping up with boiling water every 30 minutes. Once cooked, carefully remove the pudding basin, rest briefly, then turn out and serve hot with mashed potatoes and steamed vegetables.

Adaptations & Substitutions

Chilled unsalted butter instead of suet: 125 g, grated or cubed, rubbed into the flour for a tender, buttery pastry. Vegetable shortening: 125g for a slightly flakier texture.

Stuffed Roast Pork Loin

As a child, roast pork loin was a midweek treat for our family. When the joint was on the smaller side, Mum had a clever trick to make it stretch further. She would butterfly the loin and pack it with her homemade stuffing, turning a modest piece of meat into a feast for four. The result was tender pork wrapped around savoury stuffing, with plenty of flavour in every slice. It was a dish that filled both plates and bellies with no one feeling shortchanged.

Prep Time: 25 minutes   **Cook Time:** 1 hour 35 minutes   **Serves:** 4 as a main dish
Total Time: 2 hours

Ingredients

For the Pork
1kg boneless pork loin
1 tablespoon olive oil
1 teaspoon sea salt flakes

For the Stuffing
200g fresh white breadcrumbs
1 medium onion, finely chopped
2 tablespoons fresh parsley, finely chopped
1 teaspoon fresh sage, finely chopped (or 1 teaspoon dried)
1 teaspoon dried thyme
50g butter
1 egg, beaten
Sea salt and freshly ground black pepper

Method

Preheat oven to 200 °C Melt butter in a pan, add onion and cook until softened. Remove from the heat. Add breadcrumbs, parsley, sage, thyme and a good pinch of salt and pepper. Stir well. Let mixture cool slightly, add the beaten egg. Mix until stuffing is moist but not wet and holds together when pressed.

Place the pork skin-side down, slice horizontally to butterfly, keeping the meat attached.

Spread the prepared stuffing evenly over the butterflied pork loin, gently pressing it so it adheres. Roll the loin back up tightly, ensuring the stuffing stays inside, and secure with kitchen string or skewers. Rub with oil and salt and then place in a roasting tin. Roast for 20 minutes, then lower the temperature to 170 °C and cook for 1 hour 15 minutes. Rest the pork for 15 minutes before carving into thick slices with stuffing in each.

Serve with roasted potatoes or mashed sweet potatoes, a green salad or steamed vegetables, and apple or cranberry sauce if desired.

Adaptations & Substitutions

Use sourdough or whole-wheat bread instead of white for a richer flavour. Swap or add herbs such as rosemary or basil.

Stir in extras like chopped walnuts, dried cranberries or grated tasty cheese for variety. you can use a packet stuffing mix instead of homemade if you are short on time.

Storage & Reheating

Store leftovers in an airtight container in the fridge for up to 3 days. Freeze in slices for up to 3 months. Defrost in the fridge overnight before reheating in the oven, covered with foil, until piping hot.

Yorkshire Pudding

Yorkshire puddings are a British classic, always taking pride of place alongside a Sunday roast. In some homes in southern England, they are fondly called pop overs, as each pudding is "popped over" with dinner. These treats are crispy on the outside and soft on the inside, ideal for holding rich gravy and rounding off a plate. Not everyone achieves immediate success with Yorkshire puddings. Some attempts can lead to flat or soggy results. Common issues include the oven not being hot enough or opening the door too early, which can cause them to collapse. However, with the proper technique and a bit of patience, you can achieve significant results. Why stick to the usual small ones? With a bit of creativity, you can go big and use a giant Yorkshire pudding as the base for your roast dinner, filling it with your favourite meat, roasted vegetables and gravy for a memorable meal. You can also try rolling a Yorkshire pudding like a wrap.

Prep Time: 5 minutes (plus 30 minutes resting)
Cook Time: 25-30 minutes
Total Time: 30-35 minutes
Serves: 12 individual puddings (or 1 large tin as a main)

Ingredients

140g plain flour
200ml whole milk
½ teaspoon pepper
4 large eggs
½ teaspoon salt
Lard or duck/goose fat for the tins, or vegetable or sunflower oil for a plant-based option

Storage & Reheating

To keep Yorkshire puddings crisp if serving later, reheat in a preheated oven at 220 °C for 3-4 minutes. To freeze, cool completely, then transfer to a freezer-safe bag or container. Reheat from frozen in a preheated oven at 200 °C for 5-7 minutes, or until hot and crisp.

Method

Heat oven to 220 °C Add 1 teaspoon of fat or oil to each tin section
and place tin in the oven to heat.
Whisk flour and eggs together, then gradually add milk until a smooth mixture forms. Season with salt and pepper.
Let the batter rest for 30 minutes. This helps it rise, but you can skip this step if you are short on time. You can also make the batter a day in advance and store it in the fridge. Give it a good stir before using. Once the oil is hot, remove the tin and quickly pour in the batter, filling each section about two-thirds full. Pour carefully to avoid splashing. Bake for 20-25 minutes until puffed and golden.
Do not open the oven while baking.
Serve immediately with your Sunday roast, topped with gravy.

Adaptations & Substitutions

Giant Yorkshire Pudding Fillings
Classic Roast Dinner Roast beef & gravy with horseradish sauce
Sausage & mash with thick gravy
Roast chicken with sage and onion stuffing, finished with gravy
Whole Sunday roast: meat, roast potatoes, carrots, peas and gravy

Comfort Food Alternatives

Toad in the Hole: sausages in a giant pudding with onion gravy.
Shepherd's pie: minced lamb in rich gravy topped with buttery mash

Lighter Options
Creamy mushrooms & spinach with garlic sauce. Goat's cheese & roasted vegetables with balsamic drizzle
Smoked salmon & cream cheese with chives

Vegetarian & Lighter Options

Caramelised onion & Brie or Camembert Roasted
Mediterranean veg & hummus

Alternative & Fun Ideas
Chilli con carne with sour cream and coriander . Pulled pork with crunchy coleslaw. **Brunch & Breakfast Ideas.** Full English breakfast: sausages, bacon, fried egg, grilled tomatoes, baked beans scrambled eggs, crispy bacon, brown sauce or ketchup.
Eggs Benedict poached eggs, hollandaise, with ham or Smoked salmon

Yorkshire Pudding Wrap
(Adaptation)

Our bakery affectionately knew these wraps as Grandad Jack, named in honour of Carl's grandad, Jack Fox. He served Yorkshire puddings and onion gravy to officers during World War II, and one of my favourite memories was listening to him tell how they eagerly awaited their Sunday puds. At the bakery we kept that tradition alive, tucking in Cumberland sausages or roast beef, carrots, stuffing and all the classic roast trimmings. Warm, hearty and perfect for a chilly day or after a long shift, their fluffy, golden texture makes them ideal for wrapping around a roast filling.

Resting Time: 30 minutes   **Cook Time:** 18–22 minutes   **Serves:** 2–3 large wraps (serves 2 as a main)

Filling Ideas

Classic Roast
Sliced roast beef or chicken
Sage & onion stuffing
Carrots and greens
Ladle of hot gravy

Modern Market Style
Pulled pork or turkey Apple slaw Cranberry sauce Garlic mayo or onion gravy

Vegetarian
Roasted sweet potatoes
Mushrooms in red wine
Cheddar & stuffing Grandad Jack Style Cumberland sausages and onion gravy

Base Recipe

Use the Yorkshire Pudding recipe, baking in a large, flat roasting tray to a depth of about 1 cm. Bake until puffed, golden and flexible. To keep the wraps pliable, avoid overbaking and cover them with a clean tea towel as they cool slightly before filling.

Storage & Reheating

Let the wraps cool completely before storing. Wrap each in baking paper, then cling film. Freeze for up to 3 months. To reheat, defrost thoroughly, remove the cling film, re-wrap in foil and warm in a 180 °C oven for 20 minutes, or until piping hot.

Jack Fox

Curry Night In
A Takeaway at Home

Friday nights were always curry nights back home, whether it came in a foil tray from the takeaway or simmered on the hob while everyone waited with plates in hand.
These recipes bring that same comfort and colour to your kitchen, tender meats, spiced sauces, soft naan and the scent that makes the whole house feel warm. There's no need for fuss or long ingredient lists, just a few good spices, a gentle simmer and a bit of time. The result is the kind of curry that tastes even better than you remember, rich, homely and made exactly the way you like it.

Chicken Tikka Masala
Britain's unofficial national dish, tender grilled chicken simmered in a rich, spiced tomato sauce. A proper Friday-night favourite.

Lamb Rogan Josh
Deep, fragrant and warming, with slow-cooked lamb in a rich tomato and spice base, the kind that fills the kitchen with that unmistakable curry-house aroma.

Homemade Naan
Soft, pillowy and perfect for mopping up every drop of sauce, with options for garlic, coriander or sweet Peshwari.

Onion Bhajis
Golden and fragrant, just right with chutney or mint yoghurt.

British Indian
Takeaway Style Chicken Tikka Masala

Often hailed as Britain's national dish, Chicken Tikka Masala masterfully combines smoky, grilled chicken with a lush, spiced tomato sauce. Every curry house had its own version, some richer, some spicier, but all instantly recognisable. For many of us, this was the first curry we ever tried- bold yet not overpowering, comforting yet exciting. Abroad, you'll find butter chicken more often than tikka masala, but it isn't quite the same. Butter chicken is milder, sweeter and creamier, while a proper British tikka masala has more depth, tang, and that signature colour and flavour.
When you make this at home, you bring back the taste of every takeaway night in Britain, with those foil containers lined up on the table, pappadums snapping in the middle, and tikka masala proudly the star of the show.

Prep Time: 15 minutes **Marinating Time:** 2 hours (ideally overnight) **Serves:** 4 as a main
Cook Time: 45-50 minutes **Total Time:** (including 2 hours marinating) 3-3 hours

---

Ingredients

For the Chicken Marinade
600g boneless chicken breast or thigh, cut into bite-sized pieces
150g plain yoghurt
2 garlic cloves, minced
1 thumb-sized piece fresh ginger, grated
1 tablespoon lemon juice
1 teaspoon ground cumin
1 teaspoon paprika
½ teaspoon turmeric
½ teaspoon chilli powder
½ teaspoon salt

For the Sauce
2 tablespoons butter or ghee
2 onions, finely chopped
3 garlic cloves, minced
1 thumb-sized piece fresh ginger, grated
2 teaspoons ground cumin
x teaspoons garam masala
1 teaspoon paprika
½ teaspoon turmeric
½ teaspoon chilli powder (optional, for heat)
2 tablespoons tomato purée
1 x 400g tin chopped tomatoes
200ml single cream
150ml water or chicken stock
1 teaspoon sugar
Salt, to taste
Handful fresh coriander (cilantro), finely chopped, to garnish

Method

Marinate the Chicken
Mix marinade ingredients in a bowl. Add chicken, stir to coat, cover and refrigerate for at least 2 hours, ideally overnight.

Cook the Chicken
Preheat grill to high. Place chicken pieces on a grill pan or skewers. Grill for 12-15 minutes, turning once, until lightly charred and cooked through. (Alternatively, pan-fry in a hot pan with a little oil.) Set aside.

Build the Sauce
Heat butter in a large pan. Add onions and cook gently for 10 minutes until softened. Stir in garlic and ginger, cook for 2 minutes. Add cumin, garam masala, paprika, turmeric and chilli powder. Stir for 1 minute.

Continued on next page...

British Indian
Takeaway Style Chicken Tikka Masala

Simmer
Add tomato purée and chopped tomatoes. Simmer for 10 minutes to reduce. Stir in cream, water or stock, and sugar. Simmer for another 10 minutes, stirring occasionally, until thickened. Season to taste.

Combine & Serve
Add grilled chicken to the sauce. Simmer for 5 minutes to allow flavours to blend. Garnish with coriander (cilantro) and serve hot. With pilau rice and naan for the classic curry house experience. With chips, for that true British curry-and-chips indulgence. For a lighter option, pair with steamed vegetables or cauliflower rice.

Serving Suggestions
With chips, for that true British curry-and-chips indulgence. For a lighter option, pair with steamed vegetables or cauliflower rice.

Storage & Reheating
Cool completely before storing in an airtight container. Refrigerate for up to 3 days or freeze for up to 2 months. Defrost thoroughly, then reheat gently on the stove until piping hot.

British Indian Takeaway Style
Lamb Rogan Josh

If Chicken Korma was the gentle crowd-pleaser of every curry house menu, then Rogan Josh was the dish hubby ordered when he wanted something deeper and more aromatic. It always felt like the grown-up choice, a little richer, a little bolder, without blowing your head off. In Britain, every takeaway curry house seemed to have its own version, but it was always tender, slow-cooked lamb, tucked into a sauce that was both fragrant and comforting. Living abroad, Carl soon discovered that Rogan Josh doesn't always translate the same way. In some places, it turns up fiery and overpowering; in others, it arrives weak and watery, a shadow of what he remembers. That's the heartbreak of being an expat: you quickly learn that British curries really are in a league of their own. So, when the craving hits, the answer is to make it yourself.

This recipe delivers all the depth and warmth of a traditional British Indian Rogan Josh, featuring a rich tomato-based gravy and tender lamb that falls apart with a fork.

Prep Time: 15 minutes
Total Time: 40 minutes

Cook Time: 25 minutes

Serves: 4 as a main

Ingredients

For the Marinade
600g diced lamb shoulder or leg, trimmed of fat
150g full-fat plain yoghurt
1 teaspoon ground cumin
1 teaspoon ground coriander
½ teaspoon turmeric
½ teaspoon paprika
½ teaspoon salt

For the Curry Sauce
2 tablespoons oil or ghee
2 onions, finely sliced
4 garlic cloves, crushed
1 thumb-sized piece ginger, grated
1½ teaspoons ground cumin
1 teaspoon ground coriander
1 teaspoon paprika
½ teaspoon ground cinnamon
1 teaspoon garam masala
1 tablespoon tomato purée
1 x 400g tin chopped tomatoes
150ml water or beef stock
Handful fresh coriander finely chopped, to garnish

Method

Marinate the Lamb
Mix yoghurt, cumin, coriander, turmeric, paprika and salt in a bowl. Add lamb, stir well, cover and refrigerate for at least 2 hours, ideally overnight (up to 24 hours).

Brown the Lamb
Heat 1 tablespoon of oil in a heavy pan. Brown the marinated lamb in batches, then set aside. Add more oil if needed. Cook onions gently for 10–15 minutes until golden. Stir in garlic and ginger, cook for 2 minutes until soft and fragrant. Add cumin, coriander, paprika, cinnamon and garam masala. Stir for 1 minute. Mix in tomato purée and chopped tomatoes. Simmer for 5 minutes to reduce slightly. Return the lamb to the pan with the water or stock. Cover and simmer gently for 1 to 1½ hours, until the lamb is tender. Taste, adjust salt and pepper seasoning and garnish with fresh coriander. Serve with basmati rice, naan and a squeeze of lemon, if desired. Add cooling raita, a fresh salad or spicy pickles for a balanced meal.

Adaptations & Substitutions

Protein swaps: Use chicken breast, chicken thigh or beef chuck in place of lamb (cooking times will vary: chicken 30–40 minutes, beef 1½ hours). **Yoghurt alternatives:** Use low-fat or dairy-free yoghurt.

Storage

Cool completely before transferring to an airtight container. Store in the fridge for up to 3 days or freeze for up to 3 months. Defrost thoroughly, then reheat gently in a saucepan over medium heat until piping hot.

Homemade Naan

Soft, pillowy and perfectly chewy, naan is an essential accompaniment to curry in our house. It's brilliant for mopping up sauce, grabbing the last bits from the stewpan, or folding up into a wrap. My family uses them for everything: stuffed with spicy leftovers, filled with salad and grilled meat, or spread with hummus and roasted veg. Toasted or fresh from the pan, they're always helpful and always delicious. Once you've made your own, it's hard to buy them again. The best part? No fancy oven needed, just a hot pan and a few simple ingredients.

Prep Time: 15 minutes (plus 1 hour proving)

Cook Time: 10 minutes
Total Time: 1 hour 25 minutes

Serves: 6-8 Naan

Ingredients

300g plain flour, plus extra for rolling
1 teaspoon sugar
1 teaspoon salt
1 teaspoon fast-acting dried yeast
150ml warm water
2 tablespoons plain yoghurt
2 tablespoons vegetable or sunflower oil optional for brushing
Melted butter or ghee
Garlic, chopped coriander (cilantro) or nigella seeds

Storage & Reheating

Fridge: Store in an airtight container for up to 5 days.
Freezer: Layer between parchment paper, then freeze in a bag or container for up to 3 months.

Method

If using yeast that requires activation, stir it into warm water with sugar and let it sit for 10 minutes until frothy. In a large bowl, mix flour, salt, yoghurt, oil and yeast mixture to form a dough.
Turn the dough onto a lightly floured surface and knead for 5-7 minutes until smooth and elastic. It should feel slightly tacky but quite stretchy. Place dough in a lightly oiled bowl. Cover with clingfilm and leave in a warm spot for 1 hour, or until doubled in size.
Knock back the dough and divide it into 6-8 pieces.
Roll into teardrops or ovals about ½ cm thick.
Heat a heavy-based frying pan or skillet until very hot.
Cook each naan for 1-2 minutes on each side, until puffed and golden-brown spots appear. Brush with butter or ghee and sprinkle with toppings, if using.

Adaptions & Substitutions

Yoghurt: Greek yoghurt, sour cream or buttermilk all work. If thick, loosen with a splash of water or milk. **Butter or ghee:** Regular butter is fine. Mix with garlic or olive oil for extra flavour. **Garlic & Coriander Naan:** Once cooked, brush naan with melted butter or ghee mixed with 2 finely grated garlic cloves and 2 tbsp chopped fresh coriander. Serve warm.
Peshwari Naan: Before cooking, spread 1-2 tsp of a filling made from 50g desiccated coconut, 25 g ground almonds, 25 g sultanas, 1 tbsp sugar and 2 tbsp cream. Seal the dough, roll out gently, and cook as above. Brush with melted butter to finish.

Wrap It Up — Filling Ideas
Once you've mastered naan, you'll want to stuff it with everything. A few favourites: Grilled chicken, yoghurt and cucumber, for a DIY street food moment. Fried egg, crispy bacon and chutney, breakfast of champions. Halloumi, roasted veg and tahini, hearty and meat-free. Leftover roast lamb, mint sauce and salad. Sunday dinner reborn. Cheese, spinach and chilli flakes, toasted like a quesadilla. Falafel, hummus and tabbouleh, Middle Eastern-inspired goodness.

Onion Bhajis

Golden, crispy and full of spiced onion goodness, onion bhajis are an item you can't just pick up in every supermarket. Unlike samosas, they're a rare treat outside specialist shops, which is why making them at home feels like a proper indulgence. Don't worry, they're easier than you think. Perfect as a snack, starter or a cheeky nibble straight from the pan, these bhajis bring a little taste of authentic UK curry nights into your kitchen.

Prep Time: 10 minutes
Total Time: 25 minutes
Cook Time: 15 minutes
Makes: 4–6 as a side

Ingredients

2 medium onions (about 300gm), finely sliced
100g gram flour (chickpea flour)
½ teaspoon baking powder
1 teaspoon cumin seeds
1 teaspoon ground coriander
½ teaspoon turmeric
½ teaspoon chilli powder (optional, to taste)
½ teaspoon salt
Handful of fresh coriander (cilantro), finely chopped
1 green chilli, finely chopped (optional)
50–70 ml cold water (enough to bind)
Vegetable oil for deep-frying

Method

Slice onions, sprinkle with salt and set aside for 5 minutes. Add gram flour, baking powder, spices, coriander and chilli to the onions. Mix well. Stir in just enough cold water to make a thick, sticky batter, it should just hold together when pressed.
Heat oil in a deep pan to 170–180 °C (without a thermometer, drop a small piece of batter into the oil, if it sizzles and rises quickly, the oil is ready). Drop spoonfuls of the mixture into hot oil. Fry until golden brown. Remove with a slotted spoon and drain on kitchen paper.

To Serve

Best eaten hot with mango chutney or mint yoghurt Pair with curry and naan for a complete feast Add to a picnic spread or serve tapas-style with other small bites Try with a crisp cucumber and tomato salad for a refreshing contrast

Storage & Reheating

Fridge: Store in an airtight container for up to 2 days. Freezer: Freeze on a tray, then transfer to a bag or container. Keeps for up to 1 month.
Reheat: Warm in a 180 °C oven for 10 minutes from chilled, or 15 minutes from frozen, until crisp and piping hot.
Avoid microwaving, as it makes them soft.

Party Tip

Make mini bhajis by dropping teaspoonfuls of batter into oil. Serve on a platter with pots of mango chutney, mint yoghurt, or even Coronation Sauce (as featured in the sauces and pickles chapter). They make perfect canapés for a curry night or festive spread.

Bistro & Grill Favourites

Date-Night Dinners

Sometimes it's not about fancy ingredients, just simple food done well. The kind that sizzles in the pan and makes you feel like you've treated yourself. These dishes are the date-night-at-home sort: seared steaks in rich tomato sauce, garlicky lamb chops, flame-grilled burgers and crisp golden Chicken Cordon Bleu. They're made for quiet evenings in, candles lit, a glass poured, and plates that make you forget you're not out at all.

Bistecca al Pomodoro (Steak in Tomatoes)

A nostalgic Italian-style steak dish with onions, capsicum and tinned tomatoes.
A homely, sauce-soaked dinner your dad would have loved.
Best served with crusty bread or buttery mash to mop up every drop.

Flame-Grilled Burger (Big Burger Style)

Thick, juicy beef patties with all the trimmings including melted cheese, smoky bacon, crisp lettuce and a tangy relish. All the flavour of a drive-thru classic, only better.

Chicken Cordon Bleu

Tender chicken rolled with ham and cheese, crumbed and baked until golden.
Simple, elegant and far more impressive than the effort suggests.

Sticky Bourbon BBQ

Ribs Fall-off-the-bone ribs slow-cooked in a smoky bourbon and brown sugar glaze.
Sweet, sticky and irresistible, best eaten with messy fingers and good company.

Lamb Chops with Garlic & Herb Marinade

Juicy chops seared until golden, with a punchy mix of garlic, lemon and herbs that makes them sing. Perfect with roasted potatoes or a crisp green salad.

Bistecca Al Pomodoro

(Or if you don't speak Italian, Steak in Tomatoes)

This is my nostalgic nod to Dad's Friday-night special; steak simmered in tinned tomatoes. I can still see him in our kitchen at home, the air thick with the smell (and smoke) of sizzling steak and onions. The windows would steam up, the radio would play, and we'd hover nearby, waiting impatiently for his homemade chips to hit the plate. It's simple, rustic, and one of those dishes where every mouthful tastes like home.

Prep Time: 15 minutes
Cook Time: 25 minutes
Total Time: 40 minutes
Serves: 2 as a main

Ingredients

2 fillet steaks, about 2.5cm thick
2 teaspoons sea salt
1 teaspoon freshly ground black pepper
3 tablespoons olive oil, divided
2 small onions, thinly sliced
2 capsicums (peppers) of any colour, thinly sliced
4 garlic cloves, thinly sliced, or 3 teaspoons minced garlic
2 tablespoons white wine (or chicken stock if avoiding alcohol)
1 tin 400g crushed tomatoes

Method

Brush steaks with 1 tablespoon of oil and season with salt and pepper. Leave them at room temperature for 10 minutes.

Heat 1 tablespoon of oil in a large frying pan over medium-high heat. Sear steaks for 2 minutes on each side, then remove to a plate and keep warm.

Add remaining oil to the pan. Toss in onions and capsicum, season with
a pinch of salt, and cook until softened, about 8–10 minutes.

Stir in the garlic and cook for 1 minute. Deglaze the pan with white wine (or stock), scraping up the browned bits. Cook for 30 seconds until reduced slightly.

Stir in the crushed tomatoes and bring to a gentle simmer. Return the steaks to the pan and cook for 3–5 minutes, turning once, until cooked to your liking. Transfer the steaks and sauce to a serving platter. Serve immediately with crusty bread, homemade chips, or a light salad.

Adaptions & Substituions

Swap fillet steak: Rump or sirloin offer a more economical option.
Subtle Kick: Add a pinch of chilli flakes to the sauce for a subtle kick.
Italian Twist: Stir through fresh basil or oregano before serving.

Storage

It is best to eat it freshly cooked, but you can cool and cover leftovers, and keep them in the fridge for up to 2 days.
Cover and reheat in the oven 180 °C.

Flame-Grilled Burger
(Big Burger Style)

Everyone loves a good burger, whether it's from a drive-thru, a gourmet café, or a restaurant. But, you can create the perfect burger at home with just a few simple ingredients and a bit of creativity. Set the scene for a relaxed yet elevated dining experience without feeling daunted by complicated techniques.

Prep Time: 15 minutes
Total Time: 25 minutes

Cook Time: 10 minutes

Serves: 4 as a main

Ingredients

500g beef mince (regular mince is fine, but not extra lean)
4 round sesame seed burger buns (or your preferred bun)
4 slices American cheese
Lettuce leaves or shredded
1 tomato, sliced
1 onion, sliced into rings
Pickles, sliced
Burger Secret-Style Sauce (see Sauces & Pickles chapter)
1 teaspoon smoked paprika
Salt and freshly ground black pepper
Optional: crispy bacon strips, ketchup, mustard, or BBQ sauce

Method

Shape the mince into 4 equal-sized patties. Mix the smoked paprika into the mince, or sprinkle it over the patties before shaping and cooking for a smoky kick. Season both sides generously with salt and pepper. Press a slight indentation in the centre of each patty so they cook evenly.
Heat a grill, griddle, or cast-iron pan over medium-high heat. To test the mince for seasoning, cook a small piece on the grill; adjust if needed.
Cook the patties for 4-5 minutes per side, until done to your liking. Add a slice of cheese to the top of each patty in the last minute of cooking and let it melt. While the burgers cook, lightly toast the buns under the grill or in the pan until golden. Spread sauce over the two halves of the bun.

Layer in this order:
Bottom bun – lightly toasted to stop it going soggy. **Burger sauce or relish** – this soaks slightly into the bun for flavour. **Lettuce** (or another crisp element like pickles or onion), adds a barrier and crunch.
Beef patty – fresh off the pan or grill, still juicy. **Cheese** – placed on the patty while it's hot so it melts slightly. **Tomato slices or pickles** – for acidity and freshness. **Onion rings** – raw or caramelised, depending on your style. **Ketchup or mayo (optional)** – a thin layer to finish. **Top bun** – toasted and pressed gently so it all holds together. If you're going for a British-style burger, keep the lettuce below the patty (not on top) — it helps catch the juices and keeps the bun firm patty with melted cheese, lettuce, tomato, onion, and pickles. Top with the bun.
Serve with chips (fries, skin-on or curly) and a cold drink.

Adaptations & Tips

Bacon Lovers: Add crispy bacon strips for extra flavour. **Smoky Twist:** Brush patties with BBQ sauce or season with smoked salt for more depth.
Cheese Swap: If American cheese isn't available, use cheddar, Gouda, or a mild melting cheese.

Storage

Cooked burger patties will keep in an airtight container in the fridge for up to 3 days. Reheat thoroughly in a pan or the oven before serving. You can also freeze the patties (cooked or uncooked) for up to 2 months. Separate them with baking paper to stop them sticking together.

Chicken Cordon Bleu

I miss the 'DineIn' Chicken Cordon Bleu from M&S (Marks &Spencer, the British high street favourite that was famous for its posh ready meals). It was one of those easy, oven-ready suppers that felt a little more special than your average supermarket dinner. A proper staple for convenience in Britain, it was indulgent without being fussy. While I can't share their exact recipe, this version brings the same joy, tender chicken, smoky ham, gooey cheese, and a crisp breadcrumb crust baked to golden perfection.

Prep Time: 15-20 minutes
Cook Time: 20-25 minutes
Total Time: 35-45 minutes
Serves: 4 as a main

Ingredients

4 boneless, skinless chicken breasts
4 slices of ham (honey or smoked works well)
4 slices Swiss or Gruyère cheese
Salt and black pepper, to taste
60g plain flour
2 large eggs, beaten
100g breadcrumbs (fresh or panko)
30g unsalted butter
30ml vegetable oil (or more for frying Optional Creamy
Mustard Sauce
120ml double cream
1 tablespoon Dijon mustard
½ teaspoon fresh lemon juice
Salt and black pepper, to taste

Method

Preheat oven to 190 °C. Place each chicken breast between two sheets of baking paper. Gently pound with a rolling pin or meat hammer to about 1 cm thickness so they cook evenly and are easier to roll.
Lay a slice of ham and a slice of cheese on each breast, then roll up tightly to enclose.
Secure with toothpicks or kitchen string. Season with salt and pepper.
Set up a breading station with three shallow dishes, one with flour, one with beaten egg, and one with breadcrumbs. Coat each chicken roll in flour, dip in the egg, then press into the breadcrumbs until well coated.
Transfer to a baking tray and bake for 20-25 minutes, or until the chicken reaches an internal temperature of 75 °C.
For the sauce, gently heat the cream, mustard, and lemon juice in a small saucepan until smooth. Season to taste.
Remove toothpicks or string before serving. Slice into rounds or serve whole, with the creamy mustard sauce drizzled over.

Adaptations & Substitutions

Cheese Swap - Use cheddar, mozzarella, or provolone if Gruyère isn't available. **Ham Alternatives** - Try prosciutto or smoked turkey for a twist. **Lighter Version** - Skip the frying and bake instead. Lay the coated pieces on a baking tray lined with baking paper, mist with oil, and bake at 200 °C for 25-30 minutes, turning once, until crisp and cooked through.
Gluten-Free - Use gluten-free breadcrumbs and flour.

Storage

Best eaten fresh, but you can refrigerate cooked rolls for up to 2 days. Reheat in the oven until hot throughout. Not suitable for freezing once cooked.

Sticky Bourbon BBQ Ribs

Why wait for your next night out to indulge in fall-off-the-bone, sticky, sweet, and smoky BBQ ribs when you can recreate that pub or restaurant experience right at home? These Bourbon BBQ ribs are the ultimate at-home treat, delivering rich flavours and that satisfying charred, saucy finish. The sweet kick from the bourbon perfectly balances the tang of the BBQ sauce, making every bite a melt-in-your-mouth experience. Serve these beauties with crispy chips, creamy coleslaw and a chilled drink, and it'll feel like dining out at home. Perfect for a weekend get-together, a date night dinner, or any occasion that calls for something extra special.

Prep Time: 15 minutes

Cook Time: 2–3 hours (oven/BBQ) or 6–7 hours (slow cooker)

Total Time: Approx 2½–7½ hours (depending on method)

Serves: 2 as a main meal or 4 as a starter

Ingredients
2 racks of baby back ribs
8 tablespoons Bourbon BBQ Sauce
(recipe in Sauces & Pickles chapter),
Plus extra for glazing and serving Salt and pepper, to taste
Fresh parsley, chopped (optional for garnish)

Method
Prepare the Ribs Preheat oven to 150 °C or prepare your BBQ for indirect heat. Season ribs generously with salt and pepper.
Choose your cooking method
Oven method: Place ribs on a baking tray, cover with foil, and bake for 2½–3 hours until tender. BBQ method: Cook ribs over indirect heat for about 2 hours, flipping occasionally with tongs.
Slow cooker method: Place ribs in the slow cooker, cutting into sections if needed. Pour over 8 tablespoons of Bourbon BBQ sauce to coat. Cook on low for 6–7 hours until tender and meat pulls easily from the bone.

Glaze the ribs
Brush cooked ribs with more Bourbon BBQ sauce. Place back in the oven or on the BBQ and cook for 15–20 minutes, basting every 5–10 minutes until the sauce becomes sticky and caramelised.

Serve
Slice into portions, garnish with parsley if using, and serve with extra Bourbon BBQ sauce on the side.

Adaptions & Substitions
Spice it up - Add a teaspoon of cayenne pepper or smoked chilli flakes to the BBQ sauce for extra heat. **Honey Glaze** - Swap half the Bourbon BBQ sauce for honey to create a sweeter finish. **Different Cuts** - This works just as well with spare ribs or beef short ribs, adjusting cooking time as needed.

Storage & Reheating
Cool completely, then store in an airtight container in the fridge for up to 3 days. Reheat gently in the oven or microwave until hot. You can freeze it for up to 2 months.

Wine Pairing
Best with a bold, fruit-forward red such as Zinfandel, Shiraz, or Malbec, which stands up to the smoky sweetness of the BBQ sauce.

Lamb Chops with Garlic & Herbs

Mum used to serve these on Tuesdays with simple veg and gravy; it was part of a comforting routine Dad looked forward to. For this version, I've added extra herbs to lift the flavour and make the dish a little more special. Mum ran the kitchen like clockwork. Every night had its place: egg and chips on Monday, chops on Tuesday, and so on through the week. It was comforting in its predictability; you always knew what was coming. One evening, though, Dad asked if Mum could "mix it up a bit." So she did. When he sat down and saw his plate, he looked utterly baffled. "Where are the chops? I was looking forward to those!" he groaned. After that, she never strayed from the weekly menu again, and that steady rhythm became one of those small, homely traditions we all secretly loved.

Prep Time: 10 minutes (plus 1 hour marinating)
Cook Time: 15 minutes

Total Time: Approx 1-1.30 hours
Serves: 2 as a main

Ingredients

4 lamb rib or loin chops
5 garlic cloves, minced
4 tablespoons olive oil
2 tablespoons fresh parsley, chopped (or 2 teaspoons dried parsley), plus extra for garnish
2 teaspoons Tabasco Original red pepper sauce
1 teaspoon sea salt
1 teaspoon freshly ground black pepper
¼ teaspoon dried thyme
60 ml chicken or lamb stock (for pan sauce)
15g butter (for pan sauce)

Method

Combine garlic, 3 tablespoons olive oil, parsley, Tabasco, salt, pepper, and thyme in a bowl. Rub the mixture over the chops, cover with clingfilm, and refrigerate for at least 1 hour, or overnight for a deeper flavour.

Remove from the fridge 30 minutes before cooking. Heat 1 tablespoon olive oil in a heavy frying pan over high heat. Sear the chops for 2–4 minutes per side, depending on thickness.

Transfer meat to a plate, cover with foil, and rest.

Reduce heat to medium. Add stock to the pan and scrape up any browned bits that have formed on the bottom. Simmer for 2–3 minutes until slightly reduced, then stir in the butter. Season to taste.

Return the lamb to the pan to coat lightly in the sauce.

Garnish with parsley and serve with roast vegetables, mashed potatoes, or a crisp green salad.

Adaptions & Substitutions

Herb swap: Use rosemary or oregano in place of thyme.
Spicy kick: Add a pinch of chilli flakes or harissa paste.
Lighter version: Grill the chops instead of pan-frying, then drizzle with a little olive oil and lemon juice.

Storage

Leftover lamb chops will keep in the fridge for up to 3 days in an airtight container. Reheat gently in a pan with a splash of stock to keep them moist.

Little Chefs' Big Flavours

When Small Hands Meet Huge Tastes

This chapter is extra special thanks to Ava and Maisie, my two brilliant little sisters who, with a bit of help from Mum and Dad (Clair and Andrew), tested every recipe. They proved these dishes are easy enough for small hands to make, and are delicious to eat.

From crispy chicken to cheesy pasta, from burgers to flapjacks, these recipes show that homemade can truly beat the drive-thru. They're simple, delicious, and perfect for kids who want to help, or even take charge. So grab an apron (or don't, getting flour on your clothes is part of the fun), roll up your sleeves, and cook up some proper fakeaway favourites.

Whether you're a little cook or grown-up one, this chapter is about making good food, laughter, and making memories in the kitchen.

Easy Peasy Flapjacks
Chewy golden and perfect for little bakers

Cheesy Meatballs
Roll, roll for the cheesiest surprise

That's a wrap
Rolled up fun with crispy chicken and crunchy salad

Crispy Southern Fried Chicken
Crunch time chicken, no deep fryer needed

Fake-away Flame-grilled Patties
A proper nod to the fast food favourite

Lets make pizza
Your pizza, your rules, your master piece

Mac and Cheese
Creamy, cheesy and oh so delicious

Sausage and Egg Brekky Muffin
Forget the drive-through, this version is quick, tasty and less messy

Easy Peasy Flapjacks

Chewy, golden, and perfect for little bakers, flapjacks are the ultimate treat, and this version is so simple that even the tiniest bakers can get stuck in. All that is needed is just a saucepan and a spoon, no fuss. These slices are great for lunchboxes, after-school snacks, or sneaky midnight nibbles.

Prep Time: 10 minutes **Cook Time:** 20 minutes **Serves:** 12–16 bars (depending on size)

Total Time: 30 minutes

Ingredients

150g unsalted butter
150g soft brown sugar
4 tablespoons golden syrup (plus extra for drizzling, optional)
300g rolled oats
Pinch of salt
50g raisins, chocolate chips, or chopped dried fruit (optional)

Method

Pre-heat oven to 180 °C. Add the butter, brown sugar, and golden syrup into a saucepan over low heat. Stir until melted and smooth.
Remove from the heat. Stir in oats and salt. If using raisins or dried fruit, add them now. If adding chocolate chips, let the mixture cool slightly first.
Grease and line a 20cm square baking tin. Press the mixture in evenly with the back of a spoon. Bake at 180 °C for 20 minutes, until golden at the edges. For chewy flapjacks, remove when lightly golden.
For crunchier ones, bake a few minutes longer. Leave to cool in the tin, then cut into squares, fingers, or triangles.

Adaptions & Substitutions

Banana flapjacks: Mash in 1 ripe banana before baking for extra sweetness and moisture.
Nutty twist: Add 2 tablespoons of chopped nuts for crunch.
Chocolate lovers: Drizzle with melted chocolate once cooled.

Storage

Keep in an airtight tin for up to 5 days, or freeze for up to 2 months.

Cheesy Meatballs

Roll, roll, roll for the cheesiest surprise! Who doesn't love finding melted cheese in the middle of a meatball? These are perfect for kids to help make as mixing, squishing, and rolling are all part of the fun.

Prep Time: 15 minutes
Total Time: 25 minutes
Cook Time: 10 minutes
Serves: About 20 meatballs

Ingredients

500g beef mince (or turkey or chicken)
1 small onion, finely chopped
1 teaspoon garlic powder
1 teaspoon dried oregano
1 egg
50g breadcrumbs
80g mozzarella cheese, cut into small cubes
Salt and black pepper, to taste
150ml ketchup for dipping

Method

In a bowl, mix the mince, onion, garlic powder, oregano, egg, breadcrumbs, salt, and black pepper until well combined.
Kids can help with the mixing using a spoon or their hands. It's squishy but fun!
Take a small portion of the mixture and flatten it in your hand.
Place a cube of cheese in the centre, then roll the meat around the cheese to form a ball. Hide the cheese inside the meatball so none of it shows.
Heat a little oil in a frying pan over medium heat. Add the meatballs and cook for about 10 minutes, turning occasionally with tongs, until golden brown and cooked through.
Serve warm with ketchup for dipping (recipe in the Sauces & Pickles chapter).

Adaptations & Substitutions

Mini Sliders: Pop a cooked meatball into a small bun, add sliced cheese, and a squeeze of ketchup.
Extra Cheesy: Stir 2 teaspoons grated Parmesan into the meat mixture.
Oven-Baked: Cook in the oven at 200 °C for 15 minutes instead of frying.
Veggie Boost: Add grated carrot or zucchini (courgette) to the mix.

Storage & Reheating

Store cooked meatballs in the fridge for up to 3 days, or freeze for up to 2 months. Reheat thoroughly in the oven or microwave before serving.

That's a Wrap (Yo Chicken Style)

Hands-on, rolled-up fun with crispy chicken and crunchy salad. A wrap is the easiest way for kids to make their own lunch. It's tasty, colourful, and quick, plus you get to eat it with your hands (no fork required).

Prep Time: 10 minutes **Cook Time:** 7 minutes **Serves:** 4 wraps
Total Time: 17 minutes

Ingredients

500g chicken breast or thighs, cut into strips
2 tablespoons olive oil
1 teaspoon paprika
1 teaspoon garlic powder
½ teaspoon salt
½ teaspoon black pepper
4 large wraps (white or wholemeal)
1 cup lettuce, shredded
1 tomato, chopped
½ cucumber, sliced
4 tablespoons sour cream or mayonnaise (or both)
A handful of grated, tasty cheese (optional)

Method

Mix paprika, garlic powder, salt, and pepper in a small bowl.
Toss chicken strips in olive oil, then sprinkle with spices until well coated.
Heat a pan over medium heat and cook the chicken for 5–7 minutes, turning now and then, until golden and cooked through.
Lay the wraps flat. Spread a spoonful of sour cream or mayonnaise on each one.
Add lettuce, tomato, cucumber, and cheese (if using).
Top with the hot chicken strips.
Fold in the sides, roll tightly, slice in half, and tuck in.

Adaptations & Substitutions

Extra flavour: Add salsa, guacamole, or BBQ sauce.
Veggie version: Swap chicken for roasted peppers, onions, and avocado.
Lighter option: Use Greek yoghurt instead of sour cream.

Storage

Best eaten fresh, but you can keep cooked chicken in the fridge for up to 2 days and build wraps as needed.

Crispy Southern Fried Chicken
(a.k.a. Crunch Time Chicken!)

Ever wondered how fast-food joints make their chicken so crispy?
It's not magic (although it tastes like it!).
You can do it yourself with just a few simple ingredients, no deep fryer needed.

Prep Time: 15 minutes
Cook Time: 20-25 minutes
Total Time: 35-40 minutes
Serves: 4 servings

Ingredients

500g chicken (breast or thigh), cut into strips or nuggets
100g plain flour
1½ teaspoons salt
1½ teaspoons garlic powder
1½ teaspoons paprika
1 teaspoon black pepper
1 teaspoon dried oregano
1 egg
100ml milk
100g breadcrumbs (panko if possible, for crunch)
2 tablespoons vegetable oil

Method

Preheat oven to 200 °C. Line a baking tray with baking parchment and drizzle with 1 tablespoon oil.
In one bowl, mix flour, salt, garlic powder, paprika, pepper, and oregano. In another bowl, whisk the egg and milk.
Coat each chicken strip: first dredge in the flour mix, then dip in egg mix, then coat in breadcrumbs.
Place on tray, drizzle with the remaining oil, and bake for 20-25 minutes, turning halfway using tongs, until golden and cooked through.

Adaptions & Substitutions

Classic Crispy Fried Chicken-style: Skip the bread crumbs and double-dip in flour for a rougher coating.
Spicier: Add ½ teaspoon cayenne pepper or chilli powder.
Herby: Add ½ teaspoon dried thyme or sage.

Storage

It is best to eat it fresh, but store cooked chicken in the fridge for up to 2 days. Reheat in the oven for 10 minutes to crisp up again.

Fakeaway Flame-Grilled Patties
(Big Burger Style)

Because sometimes you want a big, juicy burger without queuing behind loud teenagers at the drive-thru. Thin, smoky, and made for stacking, these patties are a proper nod to the fast-food favourite. Build them up with crisp lettuce, tomato, onion, and pickles for the full fakeaway experience at home.

Prep Time: 10 minutes
Cook Time: 8–10 minutes
Chill Time: 20 minutes **Total Time:** Approx 40 minutes
Serves: 4 large patties

Ingredients

500g beef mince (premium, not extra lean)
1 tablespoon Worcestershire sauce
1 teaspoon onion powder
1 teaspoon garlic powder
½ teaspoon smoked paprika
1 teaspoon salt
½ teaspoon black pepper
1 tablespoon finely grated onion (optional)
1 teaspoon soy sauce (optional. Adds richness and browning)

Make It Fancy

Add grilled pineapple for a Hawaiian twist. Swap ketchup for chipotle mayo or melt smoked cheese on top.
Go retro with crinkle crisps and a can of Lilt on the side.

Method

Combine all ingredients in a mixing bowl. Use your hands to gently bring the mixture together without overworking it.
Shape into 4 thin, patties (they'll shrink slightly as they cook). Chill patties in the fridge for 20–30 minutes to help them hold their shape.
Cook over a hot grill or BBQ for 3–4 minutes per side until cooked through, with a flame-kissed sear.

How to Build the Burger
Toasted round sesame bun
Sliced tomato
Iceberg lettuce
Raw onion rings
Dill pickles
Ketchup & mayonnaise (spread separately, it matters!)

Adaptations & Substitutions

Beef mince: In Australia, 3-star mince gives the best juiciness. Lean mince will dry out.
Worcestershire sauce: Easy to find in supermarkets near the BBQ sauces.
Pickles: If gherkins are too sweet, look for Polish dill pickles in the continental aisle of the supermarket.
No BBQ? Use a griddle pan or cast-iron skillet for a great sear. Don't forget to make our Special Burger Sauce and Ketchup in the Sauces & Pickles chapter of this book.

Let's Make Pizza

Your pizza, your rules, your master piece. Get ready to roll, squish, stretch, and top your way to pizza greatness! This isn't just any pizza; it's your pizza. Whether you like it cheesy, veggie-packed, meat-loaded, or shaped like a smiley face, this dough is the start of something seriously delicious.

Prep Time: 20 minutes (plus 1–2 hours rising time)
Cook Time: 7–10 minutes

Serves: 2 large pizzas (or 4 smaller ones)
Total Time: Approx 1½–2 hours

Ingredients

500g strong white bread flour
1½ teaspoons salt
 teaspoon sugar
7g fast-action yeast (1 packet)
325ml warm water (not hot)
1 tablespoon olive oil (plus extra for greasing the pizza pan)

Easy Pizza Sauce
1 tablespoon olive oil
1 garlic clove, chopped
1 tin chopped tomatoes
1 teaspoon dried oregano
Salt & black pepper, to taste
Pinch of sugar (optional)
Mozzarella for topping
Basil leaves for topping (optional)

Method

Put flour in a large bowl. Add yeast to one side and salt to the other (they don't mix well at first). Stir together.
Pour in the warm water and olive oil. Mix with a spoon or your hands until a sticky dough forms. Knead on a floured surface for about 10 minutes until the dough is smooth and stretchy.
Place the dough in a lightly oiled bowl, cover with a tea towel, and leave in a warm spot for 1–2 hours, until doubled in size.
Punch down the dough, divide into two balls and flatten into a circle or roll with a rolling pin into pizza shapes on a floured surface.
Heat oil in a pan. Add garlic and cook 1–2 minutes.
Stir in tomatoes, oregano, salt, pepper, and sugar, if using. Simmer for 10–15 minutes until thickened.

Make Your Margherita
1. Spread 2–3 tablespoons of pizza sauce on the base. Top with grated or torn mozzarella. Add a few basil leaves (optional). Drizzle with olive oil.
2. Bake at 240 °C (or as hot as your oven will go) for 7–10 minutes until bubbling and golden.

RECIPE IS CONTINUED ON NEXT PAGE...

Let's Make Pizza

Pizza Fun Time – Pick Your Style!

The Cheesy Grinner – Make a smiley face with cheese, tomatoes, and olives.
Pepperoni Pals – Add mini pepperoni slices and red pepper (capsicum) shapes.
Jungle Feast – Mushrooms, spinach, and peppers (capsicum) for a veggie jungle.
Meatball Madness – Mini meatballs, red onion, and extra sauce.
Breakfast Bonkers – Scrambled egg, bacon, and cherry tomatoes for breakfast pizza!

The Science Bit (Simple & Fun)
Takeaway pizzas taste amazing because they're cooked in blazing-hot ovens that brown the cheese and puff the crust.

How to Broil Pizza (The Easy Way)
First, bake your pizza as normal at a high heat, 250 °C, for around 5–8 minutes.
Not all ovens have a broil button; it might be called "grill" instead. Just pop your pizza on the top or middle shelf so it's close to the heat coming from the top.
Then, switch your oven to "broil" or "grill" for the last 1–2 minutes.
Keep a close eye on it; this part goes fast!
You want the cheese to bubble and the crust to get those yummy golden bits, not burn.

Tip:
Grill = Broil. Same thing, different name. It's your secret trick for takeaway-style pizza at home!

Storage
You can make dough ahead, wrap it in clingfilm, and chill it for up to 24 hours or freeze it for 1 month.

Mac & Cheese

Creamy, cheesy, and oh-so-delicious, this Mac and Cheese is comfort food at its best. Forget the packet stuff; this is homemade, simple, and guaranteed to put smiles around the table.

Prep Time: 10 minutes **Cook Time:** 20 minutes **Serves:** 4
Total Time: 30 minutes

Ingredients

250g elbow macaroni (or any pasta shape)
25g butter
25g plain flour
250 ml milk
200g grated cheddar cheese
1 teaspoon mustard (optional, for zing)
Salt and black pepper, to taste
50g breadcrumbs (optional, for topping)

Method

Bring a pot of salted water to the boil, add the pasta, and cook according to packet instructions. Drain, reserving a splash of cooking water.
In a saucepan, melt butter over medium heat. Stir in flour to make a paste. Gradually add milk, whisking until smooth and thick.
Add grated cheese and stir until melted into the sauce. Season with salt, pepper, and mustard (if using). Stir the cooked pasta into the sauce until well coated. If it's too thick, loosen with a little pasta water.
Optional crispy topping: Spoon pasta into an oven-proof dish, sprinkle with breadcrumbs, and bake at 180°C for 10 minutes until golden and bubbling.

Adaptations & Variations

Bacon boost: Stir in crispy bacon bits. **Veggie mac:** Add peas, sweetcorn, or broccoli florets. **Hot dog mac:** Slice in frankfurters for a retro twist. **Extra cheese:** Top with mozzarella or parmesan before baking.

Storage

It is best to eat fresh, but you can keep leftovers in the fridge for up to 2 days and reheat them in the oven or microwave.

Sausage & Egg Brekky Muffin

The break fast boss challenge in a bun. Forget the drive-thru; this homemade version is quick, tasty, and less messy. Baking the eggs in a muffin tin gives you the perfect round shape to fit snugly into your English muffin, before adding sausage or bacon to finish it off.

Prep Time: 5 minutes
Total Time: 20 minutes

Cook Time: 15 minutes

Serves: 2 muffins

Ingredients

2 English muffins
2 sausages
(or 2 rashers of bacon)
2 eggs
2 slices cheddar cheese
1 tablespoon butter
(for toasting)
Salt and black pepper,
to taste

Method

Slice the muffins in half. Heat a pan with butter and toast the muffins cut-side down until golden.
Preheat oven to 180 °C. Grease a muffin tin and crack one egg into each cup. Season with salt and pepper. Bake for 10–12 minutes, until egg whites are set (cook longer if you like firm yolks).
Remove sausages from their skins and flatten into patties. Fry in a pan for 5–7 minutes until golden and cooked through.
For bacon, fry 3–4 minutes each side until crisp. Drain on a paper towel.
Place a slice of cheese on the bottom half of each muffin. Add the sausage patty or bacon, top with the baked egg, then finish with the muffin lid.
Eat like a champion: Press lightly to squash it together, then take a big bite of breakfast joy.

Adaptations & Substitutions

Go fancy: Add avocado slices or fresh tomato. **Extra kick:** A splash of hot sauce under the cheese. **Veggie swap:** Use a veggie sausage patty instead.

Storage

Eat them fresh; however, you can make cooked patties and baked eggs ahead and store them in the fridge for a day.

About the Author

Linda Davey is a British-born food writer and creator of Pork Pies & The Perfect Pickle, a cookbook celebrating the flavours of home for British expats living abroad. Now based in sunny Perth, Australia, she spends her days recreating the comforting dishes she grew up with, from pork pies and sausage rolls to puddings that taste like Sunday afternoons at Mum's table.

Before turning her hand to writing, Linda ran a small bakery in Western Australia, where she shared her love of honest, hearty British food with locals who couldn't resist a proper pasty. Her writing blends storytelling, memory, and gentle humour, offering readers both practical recipes and a reminder of home. When she's not cooking or writing, you'll find her pottering in the garden, testing new condiments for her farmhouse pantry range, or planning her next community event, always with a wooden spoon in one hand and a cup of tea in the other.

Notes For The Reader

All rights reserved. No part of this publication may be reproduced, stored in a retrieval system, or transmitted in any form or by any means, electronic, mechanical, photocopying, recording, or otherwise, without the prior written permission of the author.

The information in this book is based on personal experience and research. While every effort has been made to ensure accuracy, the author and publisher assume no responsibility for errors or omissions, or for any loss, injury, or damage caused by the use or misuse of the information or recipes contained herein.

All recipes have been tested in a domestic kitchen. Results may vary depending on ingredients, equipment, and individual cooking methods. Always check product labels for allergens and dietary information.

Linda x

www.ingramcontent.com/pod-product-compliance
Lightning Source LLC
Chambersburg PA
CBHW061804290426
44109CB00031B/2934